DESIGNER FAUX finishing

QUARRY

DESIGNER FAUX finishing

ideas and inspiration for Sophisticated Surfaces

VICTOR DeMASI

BEVERLY MASSACHUSETTS

QUARRY BOOKS

© 2008 by Quarry Books

First published in the United States of America by
Quarry Books, a member of
Quayside Publishing Group
100 Cummings Center
Suite 406-L
Beverly, Massachusetts 01915-6101
Telephone: (978) 282-9590
Fax: (978) 283-2742
www.quarrybooks.com

Library of Congress Cataloging-in-Publication Data

DeMasi, Victor.
  Designer faux finishing : ideas and inspiration for sophisticated surfaces / Victor DeMasi.
     p. cm.
  ISBN 1-59253-347-7
  1. Painting. 2. Decoration and ornament. 3. Finishes and finishing. I. Title.
  TT385.D466 2008
  745.7'23--dc22

                                                                     2008014898
                                                                        CIP

ISBN-13: 978-1-59253-347-3
ISBN-10: 1-59253-347-7

10 9 8 7 6 5 4 3 2 1

Design: Sandra Salamony
Cover Image: Randy O'Rourke

Printed in Singapore

dedication

To my wife, Roanna, and daughters, Mercedes and Orianna,

who have been my biggest cheerleaders through the years

contents

a note on faux:
a short history of faux painting

Thirty years ago, I concocted my first glaze, creating a broken-wall-color effect. It was an eye-of-newt, toe-of-frog effort based on vague recipes and descriptions gleaned from a Victorian painter's text. The noxious, linseed-oil fumes of my early stipples and scumbles drove people from their houses, and caused headache-induced rebellions among my finishers. Back then, paint store shelves were not lined with environmentally friendly products, nor were there design-technique books illuminating the best methods and recipes. I made it up as I went along. Before there was such a trend as "faux," I was simply called a house painter.

In the 1980s, homeowners began to plumb the past for their decorating guidance and inspiration. The Victoriana craze found new value in old houses. Wide trim-work detailing and ornate embellishment were prized, eclipsing the white, bare-bones interiors of modernism. Painters started to fancy things up, using simple techniques such as sponging and rag-painting for simple finishes. Their skills multiplied with the decades, and revolutionary paint formulas flooded the market for creating "paint magic," a term made famous by Jocasta Innes's book of the same name. Those products expanded the possibilities for decorating surfaces, but also created a profusion of complicated methods and mixtures. A proliferation of books and magazine features spread the faux-painting message. Consumers and homeowners accepted—even embraced—the option of decorating surfaces with paint techniques. A virtual army of artisans grew in ranks and experience to meet the market's needs.

By the mid-1990s, artisan networks, many new painting schools, and the demands of style were driving innovation in painted finishing. Creative workers began layering simple techniques to produce more complex options. Murals became more common, and their popularity fed a taste for hand-painted borders and innovative use of stencils. The stereotypical image of country-style, cow-and-chicken stencils was left behind. Gilding became more affordable with the development of revolutionary mica paints that recreate a metallic surface with relative ease. A new golden age of paint for interior decoration had arrived.

All these techniques are considered faux painting. Today's faux painter falls along the spectrum somewhere between housepainter and interior designer. Faux painting styles will continue to evolve as the Internet and travel abroad increases homeowners' exposure to painted finishing ideas around the globe. Decorative-paint artisans regularly gather and network at conventions where ideas, skills, and techniques are shared. Thus, it is the perfect time for a book that curates some of the best work from the world of international faux finishing.

The Elements of Painting Style

A few themes emerge from this survey that guide and suggest the elements of well-considered finishes, but are not to be considered rigid rules for design. Ultimately, as with most art, beauty is in the eye of the beholder, and personal taste dictates the finishes that are most pleasing and evocative.

Color is almost everything. Without a strong sense of color, even the savviest techniques will fail to inspire. Good color choice can fortify weak technique, but poor color choice will undermine even the strongest technique.

Simple methods can create a strong finish. Even the simplest color-washes made from the local hardware store's paint supply can be used to create a sophisticated wall finish. Compelling design can be deceptively straightforward.

Complex results arise from the layering of simple methods. An unlimited number of techniques can be combined, depending on the creativity of the artisan. Metallic paint stenciled as damask over a color-washed wall represents three layers: base paint, glazing wash, and stencil application. With each multilayered effect, faux painting can enter the realm of art.

A paintbrush is only as good as the painter wielding it. A fortune spent on specialty tools will not create a designer finish. Aspiring painters will benefit more from practice, direction, and experience with color than from a pricey arsenal. Usually, basic tools create dramatic effects.

Each room of the home has its own decorating needs. Baths, entries, cabinets, and trim with durable finishes age well. Bedrooms encourage rest with soft, cool color schemes. Dining rooms painted the color of rare meat will not encourage the appetite. Consider the flow of color and finishes from one area or room to another; the color scheme for a dwelling is best considered as a whole before the parts are decorated.

Navigating This Book

Part I examines how tools and paints are used to decorate a room. The discussions are not meant to be an exhaustive review but rather to highlight the basic building blocks of faux finishing. It is a simple start for what can become a very involved undertaking.

Part 2 includes detailed sections on popular faux finishing techniques. Each section introduces a gallery of recent projects by professional faux finishers. Stunning photos illustrate grand treatments of living spaces, as well as more modest examples. Artist profiles highlight the international creativity that informs the twenty-first-century painted home. Tutorials in each section teach the techniques used to create the painted effects.

As the book progresses, the projects become more challenging and time consuming. Yet all the techniques use the same basic materials introduced in the first part of the book, unless otherwise noted. The creative reader is encouraged to experiment with combinations and variations. The homeowner shopping for renovation ideas can use this book as a guide when contracting finishers. Artisans who contributed to this effort are all listed at the end, and are available for projects, so please visit their websites.

Generic names are used for all the materials and products in this book. It would be impossible to catalog in one book the bewildering selection of painting products on the market, but a local paint retailer should be able to offer modest insight on them. Good information can also be found on the products' labels and the manufacturer's websites, and at professional-level workshops. Resources, page 170, reveals a few of the products I often use, more out of familiarity than superiority. Artisans tend to be conservative in their choice of materials; I use again what has worked before.

Designer Faux Finishing is part showcase, part tutorial, and part inspirational painting handbook. Let's get painting!

Vincent O. DeMasi

paints and painting formulas

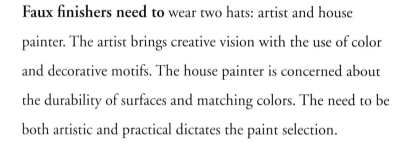

Faux finishers need to wear two hats: artist and house painter. The artist brings creative vision with the use of color and decorative motifs. The house painter is concerned about the durability of surfaces and matching colors. The need to be both artistic and practical dictates the paint selection.

A complete review of paint materials and their uses can be overwhelming. For those who enjoy the research, reviewing literature and painting traditions will provide many options for faux finishing. A novice need not know all ways, just one or two ways that work. Every painter has his own favorite mixtures.

This red Venetian plaster finish is applied in multiple steps and burnished to a high sheen by rubbing vigorously with a steel taping knife.

History of Decorative Painting

Historical archives chronicle paint recipes onward from the Renaissance. While the methods and motifs traditionally used in painted decoration are of great interest, little of the information on paints older than twenty years remains useful, except for conservation artists. In fact, many paints once in common use are no longer available.

A Greener Faux Finish

Concerns about air quality and pollutants in our environment are pushing many governments to curtail the use of petroleum in paint manufacturing. Oil-base paints, solvents, and media, so popular with faux finishers in the recent past, are increasingly harder to obtain. Their disposal is also an expanding cost factor, as municipalities move to control hazardous waste.

Many consumers aware of this trend are reluctant to use petroleum products on their projects. Yet oil-base primers and glazes remain important tools in the preparation and decoration of houses.

glaze's colorful past

Dutch masters in Rembrandt's time introduced glazes in their oil paintings. They mixed small amounts of pigments into linseed oil and applied the transparent washes to their canvases, softening bright colors. Canvas painters also painted houses in those times, and they tried similar glaze on marbleized doorframes and moldings.

Imitation of wood, called *graining*, (*faux bois* in French) evolved in England after the Great Fire of London in 1666. Residential construction with oak was forbidden by royal decree to reserve the decimated inventory for shipbuilding. Painters and stainers found a market eager for imitated oak grain.

Huguenot refugees fleeing religious persecution in Europe also carried wood graining and marbleizing traditions to the New World, popularizing the skills in the Boston area.

Historically, stale beer, vinegar, linseed oil, and other agents were mixed with paint pigments to make glazes, although many recipes were secrets taken to the grave. Those formulas that survive are largely curiosities; manufactured glazes have eased the efforts of contemporary faux finishers.

Clouds in this ceiling treatment are softly blended using water-base glazes, which have quick drying time that allows the painter to work without interruption on this complicated project.

Good ventilation and personal protection such as respirators and gloves make using oils a safe option. Still, there's no denying the change in materials and hazard reduction through the elimination of petroleum solvents.

Beginning in the 1980s, air-quality regulations pushed manufacturers to begin substituting water-base products wherever possible. Early success with latex house paints led to a water-base revolution.

Attempts at "latex" varnishes (clear finishes) performed poorly at first, but improved over time.

Water-base glaze evolved in the 1990s. One could then mix water-base interior house paint or artists' acrylic paint with newly introduced "latex" glaze, and confidently decorate over latex-base coats. A wall-glazing job that would have been done with oil two decades before could be done completely in water: base coat, glaze, and varnish.

Demand for decorative paint finishes in the home continues to force innovation in the faux-finishing world, as well as in the paint trade overall. Radical changes in the last twenty years point to a very green faux environment. Despite the claims, however, caution about the safety of water-base materials is advised. Many of the new chemicals in paints have scarcely been studied for hazards.

Paint Bases

Decorative painters need to be familiar with interior house paints for two reasons: these paints provide the base coat, or ground, for a painted effect; and they are mixed into glazes to provide the actual decoration.

Paint selection is often a personal preference of the worker, especially those who come from an artistic, not a trade, background. A multitude of selections, including artist oil paints, gouache, and Japan colors, can be used with success in faux finishing. Their review in many books on the subject adds drama to the paint discussion. This book limits discussion of the illustrated techniques to the paint and media commonly found at a well-stocked paint supplier. A skilled finisher can use these products for results of the highest order.

OIL-BASE PAINTS

Oil-base finish paints, primers, and glazes use mineral spirits as their solvent. They are commonly called *alkyds* for the resins used in their manufac-

turing. They are considered more hazardous to use because of their noxious fumes and ability to cause skin irritation.

Oil-base paints are seldom used on walls, except as primers. They make excellent hard enamels for trim work, where they continue to be used in many high-end homes. Oil-base trim paints level nicely after being painted, making for a smoother surface. They also dry slowly and have high adhesion to most surfaces, making for less prep work and fewer primer coats. In addition, slow drying enables easy cleanup and correction of mistakes. Faux finishers value oil-base glazes for the long "open time" they allow for working on techniques such as stippling or antiquing.

WATER-BASE PAINTS

Water-base—or waterborne—paints, primers, and glazes use water as a solvent.

Latex, a milky tree resin from tropical Asia, was formulated as a water-base house paint in the 1950s. Seldom used today in paints, latex persists as a generic description of water-solvent house paints. *Acrylic* and *vinyl* better describe many of the products (and their properties) sold in the paint store as latex. The terms *latex* and *water-base* are used interchangeably throughout this book for general descriptions of water-solvent media.

oil and water

In most cases, oil-base paints will "stick" to anything. Oils can be painted over other paints with little concern for adhesion failure—the great fear of all house painters. Oil-glaze mediums have the same dependable grab.

Applying water-base paint over oil-painted surfaces will result in adhesion failure: water-base paint rolls up into little balls and stringy lumps. When dry, the latex paint can be easily scraped off with a fingernail. Water glazes have the same adhesion problems.

Furniture, cabinets, and trim work are likely places to find oil-base paints in the home. This is especially true in older homes, which may retain their treatments from the era when oil-base ruled.

"Oil over water, but not water over oil" is the house painter's credo, and this caution is best observed by the faux finisher as well.

COMPATIBILITY TEST

When in doubt, paint or glaze a small test area, allow it to dry completely, then put some masking tape on the area and rip it off quickly. If the masking tape takes the new paint film with it, there is an adhesion problem. Extra preparation such as sanding and using a primer is advised.

Latex paints are characterized as fast drying, which allows for quick recoating of house paints, or moving along to the next step of a faux finish glaze. Surface preparation is often critical for latex paints because of their poor adhesion. They are valued as user-friendly with easy cleanup, but many problems arise from painters confusing the ease of cleanup with the surface preparation, which is never easy.

Fluid acrylic paints from the artist market are also finding wider use by faux finishers. These are essentially the pasty, tube paints formulated in a liquid state similar to latex house paints. They are well-suited for hand-painting techniques such as murals and borders, and mix readily into house paints to alter colors. Because of their higher cost, however, they are less practical when large quantities of material are needed.

MICA PAINTS (METALLICS)

Micas are a recent innovation in water-base paints that deserve special mention. Mica is a nonmetallic imitation of metal, which replaces the highly-toxic bronzing powders previously used for gilded effects. Micas do not rival the brilliance achieved by the expensive process of gold leafing, but they do provide exciting possibilities for creating a metallic look, especially on large areas such as walls and ceilings.

OTHER FAUX OPTIONS

A large selection of faux products confronts the shopper at retail and mail-order outlets. Venetian plasters and texture paints clean up with water but do not shoehorn easily into the water-base category popularized by latex paint.

A product such as iron paint is water based, but needs a special primer and a final wash with dangerous acids to achieve the rust effect. One should hesitate to assume that a manufacturer's water-base classification makes it safe or easy to use.

Faux painting product lines available through mail-order outlets offer exciting possibilities in painting decoration. Some finishes are unique to the distributor, but most can be achieved with materials available from a well-stocked paint store. With decorative product lines, follow the steps

A platinum metallic paint was applied on moldings and over anaglypta-embossed wall covering.

This ceiling treatment, which originated in Damascus, dates back to the Ottoman Empire and was rendered without the aid of modern technology. Geometric motifs are typical in Islamic art where depiction of man or beast is forbidden.

SANDING REQUIRED

Many primer-sealer directions claim no need for sanding. Don't believe it! A fine sandpapering—also called rubbing—on woodwork, cabinetry, and floors doubles the insurance against adhesion failure, and smoothes the surface for greater beauty. Nobody likes prep work, but spare the primer and sandpaper, and you'll spoil the project.

closely on the manufacturer's accompanying literature. Beware that many products are offered with little useful information. Consider attending workshops or personal instruction if you are interested in more specialized product lines.

ALCOHOL-BASE PAINT

The solvent for shellac is alcohol; it's noxious, but the powerful odor dissipates quickly.

Shellacs are varnishlike finishes that trigger memories of Grandma's shiny furniture ("It's shellacked," she used to say). Shellac is also an important pigmented interior paint. White shellac paints are used widely in interiors as fast drying, high-adhesion primers, which can be immediately recoated to build an opaque film. They offer poor resistance to water and alcohol, which will dissolve them.

LACQUER-BASE PAINT

These specialized paints and clear finishes are popular in cabinet shops. They are quick drying and are mostly applied with spray equipment. Excellent at leveling, lacquers paint those ebony piano finishes, which astound with their deep, black shine.

Lacquer solvents are extremely toxic and seldom of use to the faux finisher. Since a great deal of cabinetry and some trim work are finished with lacquer paint, decorative painters sometimes need to repaint them with faux techniques. Most oil formulas, but not water-base mediums, will adhere to lacquer.

Clear Finishes

Varnish and polyurethane are clear finishes that protect and enhance faux finishes.

Varnish is a traditional word, referring to an oil-base finish that is seldom used today. The term persists as a generic description for clear finishes, much as latex generically describes water-base house paints.

A damask-inspired pattern sits naturally on a soft, stippled ground which was created with single-process glazing technique.

why use a primer-sealer?

Primer paint prepares a surface for a finish, ensuring a good job. It guarantees adhesion when changing a surface from oil-base paints to water-base, latex paints. Primer is mandatory on all raw surfaces being painted for the first time, such as wood, drywall, and plaster.

Many primers are also called sealers for their ability to seal undesirable features of the surface material. Natural oils that migrate out of soft lumber, such as cedar and pine, will discolor a finish, so it's best to seal it. Bleed-prone aniline dyes, which are popular on furniture and stained woodwork, need to be sealed when those surfaces are to be painted. Heavy odors remaining in a smoker's rooms or fire-damaged areas also qualify for a sealer.

Primer-sealers enhance the appearance of the base. They even out repaired spots, minimize lapping, and allow finish coats to spread further by controlling absorption. A base coat over a primer-sealer ensures success on more complicated faux finishes. Additional stenciling and striping steps involve taping over the base coat. Removing the tape often lifts the base coat on poorly adhered coats, and ripping can be extensive. A primer-sealer coat ensures the base coat adhesion, saving laborious touchup, which never looks as good as if there was no damage in the first place.

TINTED PRIMER

Consider tinting a primer for better treatment of the decorative surface. Midtone and dark base coats will achieve better coverage, saving time and material. No matter how many coats are applied, bold saturated colors will be more vibrant if painted on a tinted base coat.

achieving the wet look

Furniture makers use sprayed lacquer finishes to impart a deep, clear dimension to their work; a film of water seems to lie on the surface. A similar appearance on marbleized trim work, or on walls finished in subtle glazing techniques, can be obtained by following the faux finish with four to six coats of gloss-sheen, water-base varnish. These materials dry quickly, allowing multiple coats to be applied in a reasonable period of time. Be sure to completely prepare the surface, as the glass-like result highlights even the smallest imperfections.

Clear finishes are necessary on faux-finished trim work, floors, and cabinetry, which are subject to high traffic. Most faux finishes on walls and ceilings do not need clear finishing, but varnish can enhance these surfaces by creating greater depth.

One coat of "latex varnish" on trim provides a silky feel, whereas three coats add a look more suited for furniture. In some cases, a clear finish can also be used strictly for enhancement, such as to create a wet look that imitates a lacquered surface.

Stir varnish and polyurethane before and frequently during use. Flattening agents added to dull the sheen of these finishes tend to settle to the bottom of the container. If you do not mix them in well, you will create an uneven sheen across the surface.

Never shake a can of clear finish. This will result in trapped air bubbles that pop out as the finish dries, leaving ugly craters. Varnish large areas quickly, using a short-nap roller, and top the wet film with brush strokes to eliminate air-bubble cratering.

OIL VARNISHES

Oil polyurethanes are widely used, especially in floor finishing. Like oil-base products, polyurethanes (also called *polys*) tend to *amber*, or turn yellow as they dry. This ambering enhances many wood-stained colors, and aids the faux finisher's final step in wood-graining projects and aged-antique effects. Ambering alters the appearance of a faux finish considerably, and is undesirable over soft pastel colors.

Oil polys, unlike other solvent-based products, have poor adhesion on some surfaces, causing them to flake off after use. They are especially tough and scratch resistant, explaining their continuing popularity on floors. Leave many hours for sufficient drying between coats.

WATER VARNISHES

Latex clear finishes are the first choice for today's painter. Unlike latex paints, they adhere to most surfaces, making them useful over oil-base faux finishes as a final step. They are very sensitive to humidity and temperature, especially cool conditions, which might cause a cloudy bloom of trapped water vapor in the varnish film. The only cure for this worst of painting disasters is a complete reapplication of the finish, from step one.

READ THE CAN

You can learn a lot by reading the back of a can before opening it—instead of later, when it comes time for problem solving. This is especially true for faux finishing products.

SHELLACS AND WAX

Clear and amber alcohol-base shellacs were popular in the Victorian era. The once-mainstay finish appears blackened on old house floors and furniture, demanding complete removal. However, with their great adhesion—even on glass—and their instant drying, shellacs remain a minor but useful product on the painter's shelf.

Waxes are finding renewed popularity in some faux-finishing circles. Waxes buff to a beautiful deep sheen as a finish coat for Venetian plasters. Wood-colored waxes provide an aged look for antiqued surfaces.

Shellac-wax finishing enjoys continuing popularity in the antique trade, and should be considered by faux finishers of furniture projects.

Choosing a Base Coat

All painted finishes start with a base coat, or ground. The resulting finish is affected by the solvent base of the paint; its sheen and color; and the care that goes into preparing the surface. Mistakes and corner-cutting in the early steps of finishing often lead to problems, which could mean repeating all the steps.

SHEEN

Glazing techniques require several ample base coats of quality paint (with sheen) to prolong the open time of the glaze concoctions.

The sheen of paint is defined by its reflectivity and appearance, while the base of paint describes its solvent. This is an important difference which

Base coats are applied with standard brush and roller tools.

quality considerations

House painters favor flat-sheen formulas for walls to minimize the appearance of defects, such as dings and patches. This cuts their preparation time. Flat paint is the most common paint found on walls. It is the most economical of paints, with some very cheap versions common especially in new construction. These "builders' paints," inferior in durability and adhesion, are best primed and repainted with a better-quality product.

Better-quality paints are advertised as washable, but this does not mean they're easy to clean. It means they cannot be washed off the walls. Take some warm soapy water on a sponge and gently scrub a wall. If the paint washes off, it is nonwashable. Nonwashable paint is unsuitable for a time-consuming faux finish, and should be base-coated again, first with a primer-sealer and then with a quality paint before proceeding.

This expertly painted Swedish-style wall panel demonstrates the mastery of many glaze techniques.

should not be confused. Flat, eggshell, and semi-gloss are common sheens for both oil-base and water-base interior paints.

FLAT

A flat paint has no sheen, whereas a high-gloss has the most, and a range of sheens exist in between. The sheen of paint determines its use as a base coat in faux finishing. Traditional house-painting rules go a modest way in advising decorative finishers on what to use.

Flat paints are very absorbent, and are inadequate bases for glazing effects such as dragging, color-washing, and ragging. They absorb glazes too quickly, and allow none of the open time necessary to work the material on the surface. A flat sheen can be used successfully for some faux finishes that do not use glazing techniques, such as murals, painted borders, and pebbling.

EGGSHELL, SATIN, AND MATTE

These paint sheens provide low luster, subtly reflective surfaces that differ in small increments from one another. Higher in quality than flat paints and more expensive, they are good base coats for glazing techniques.

SEMIGLOSS AND GLOSS

Semigloss and gloss are good choices for trim and other high traffic areas because they provide a hard enamel surface that is attractive and easy to clean, but their high reflectivity does show imperfections.

As the sheen of paint increases, it becomes more difficult for other paints to adhere to it. Glaze mixtures have this same problem, tending to slide off a high-sheen ground and releasing if a clear finish is later applied. Do not choose high-sheen paint for a base coat, and thoroughly sand with fine paper any existing glossy surface that is to be decorated with a paint technique.

OTHER CONSIDERATIONS FOR BASE COATS

Every faux finish requires careful consideration of the base coat. Determine the color and sheen you want by making samples. The examples below explain how the nature of the ground varies with the finish.

For Venetian plaster finishes, flat- or low-sheen paint provides a suitable ground. The color of the ground is very important, and must be close to the finished color of the plastering. A white ground beneath a deep burgundy plaster will scream in high contrast wherever the plaster cover thins. For the ground, tint a flat acrylic paint to approximate the color of the polished plaster.

Gold-leaf work needs a higher sheen for the ground. Sizing, which adheres the leaf to the ground much like glue, absorbs quickly on a lower sheen, causing the thin leaves of gold to flake off later. The ground must be colored to deep yellow or terra-cotta—traditional colors for leafing.

Unlike leaf, metallic paints adhere best to flat paints. To save extra coats of these expensive paints, tint the base coat to approximate the color of the metallic finish. Beware of any suggestion to use a primer-sealer for a base coat. Not all primers dry flat; some dry with a fair amount of sheen, which will reduce adhesion of a metallic paint, and cause problems later if tape is placed on the surface for decorative effects.

CUTTING IN CORNERS

When applying a latex base coat, always cut—paint—the edges and corners with a brush before roller painting the wall. The roller's texture differs from the brush, and rolling as close as possible to edges and corners after brush cutting creates a more uniform base coat texture.

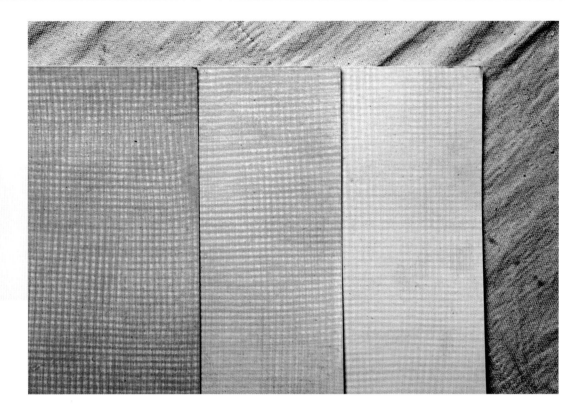

Glazes are necessary to make these broken color techniques.

Making a Transparent Color Glaze

Glazing liquids dry transparently if they are not colored (tinted) by paint or pigment. They are rarely applied straight from the can, except as a protective layer over a decorative technique. Colorants and solvents are usually added to glazing liquids to create a tinted concoction. Such concoctions are then used to create the soft or bold faux finishes featured throughout this book. Different glazing products have very different personalities; faux finishers become very attached to their own brand of glazing liquids and the concoctions they make with it.

SUPER STRAPPER

Oil glazes are far superior to water glazes in strapping down to all surfaces. Use oil glazes over all base coats, whether oil, latex, or lacquer. Water glazes adhere best to latex and shellac grounds.

As a painting method, glazing simply means applying a glaze over a base coat, and then distressing it with a technique such as ragging, dragging, or stippling. Marbleizing, wood-graining, and faux stone are more complicated glazing techniques.

All glazing techniques require a high-quality, sheen paint for the base coat. Because flat paint is absorbent, attempts to apply a glaze finish over it will result in a disagreeable, muddied appearance. A basic faux finishing rule is *no glazing over flat paint.*

The commercial glazing liquids used in this book are colored by the addition of lesser quantities of paint to make a glaze concoction. These concoctions are applied over a base coat by brush, roller, or sponge. For a short length of time, known as *open time,* the concoctions float on the surface and can be manipulated (distressed) with a tool: brush, comb, rag, or even fingers. Open time is a quality greatly prized by finishers; more open time allows for more possibilities in technique.

A distressed glaze should be left to dry. However, it may not *strap down,* or adhere to the base coat, for several days. If a glaze is varnished before strapping down, it may reliquify and release. Like paints, glazing liquids come in oil and water bases. Always observe the no-water-over-oil rule in glazing endeavors.

WINDOW OF OPPORTUNITY

The difference between open time, which is the window of workability, and strap down, which is the grab to the base coat, are important features of any glaze concoction.

As a general rule, water glazes have less open time than oils, making some finishes— particularly strie and wall combing—difficult to execute. Water-glaze concoctions that have a longer open time sacrifice adhesion to the base, making follow-up coats of clear finish problematic. Although water-base glazes dominate today's market, oil-glaze concoctions still have a place.

Finishing cabinets requires a long open-time glaze for strie work. Use an oil glaze that straps down overnight, and then a protective varnish the next day. An oil glaze can also be used for subtle stippling on a wall job that is slated to receive several coats of varnish for a wet-look, lacquer effect.

Use a water glaze for color-washing walls that do not need a protective clear finish and will receive stenciled borders. You can also use a water glaze on a high ceiling that no one will ever touch.

KNOW VARNISH FROM GLAZE

Making and applying glazes are the most important skills of the faux finisher. Do not confuse varnishes, particularly the glossy ones, with glazes. Glazes have color added. A varnish can be made into a glaze by the addition of small amounts of paint or pigment, but it no longer stands as a clear finish.

RESCUING GLAZE

A skin will form on a partially used can of oil glaze, even when it is stored for a short period of time. Rescue these expensive solvent-based products by mixing the skin with a small amount of paint thinner until it is lique-fied again. Strain the mix through cheesecloth into a clean container, then use.

glazed over

It's easy to tint glazes by adding modest amounts of interior house paints. Use latex paints for water-base glazes and oil-base paints for oil concoctions.

• Fluid acrylic artist paints can be used to color small amounts of glazes for small projects, such as furniture and murals.

• Most oil glazes dry with a matte sheen, regardless of the paint added. They are slow-drying, soft, and poor in durability, making an extra step of protective varnish more desirable.

• Water glazes generally dry to the sheen of the paint and the glazing liquid, which ranges from satin to gloss.

• Substitute thicker wood stains for house paints to color glaze concoctions, when a wood color is desired for graining techniques.

tools and techniques

Thoreau said it best: simplify. Always use a simple approach when planning your painted finish. Novices err on the side of making things complicated. Skilled faux finishers reach into a toolbox of simple applicators such as rags, combs, or an old brush to distress glaze concoctions. The skill is in the hand, not the tool.

Simple-process finishes can be combined and layered for visually complex results. You can add stenciling over a simple-process finish, or tape areas and faux-finish borders for stunning decoration.

brushes and applicators

The general *old-time* rule is to use animal-bristle brushes for oil paints and synthetic bristles for water-base mediums. New materials mean some new rules. Synthetic bristles, such as Chinex on larger house-painter brushes and Taklon on artist brushes, handle both mediums adequately. Painters choose brushes mainly according to personal preference. Never be afraid to experiment until you find a comfortable brush.

Avoid spending freely for exotic-looking brushes and gadgets until you understand the true need. A special brush can meet a need, but on most occasions, the skill of the artisan—not the tool—determines the quality of the finish.

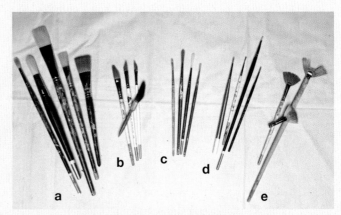

Artist's brushes for detail work. The synthetic bristles can be used with oil-base or water-base mediums.

ARTIST'S BRUSHES FOR DETAIL WORK

a. General purpose flat and mop brushes

b. Dagger stripers for floral work and marbleizing

c. Pencil stripers for stone grouting

d. Pointers for detailing

e. Fans for softening glazes in corners

BRUSHES FOR LARGE PROJECTS

a. Synthetic Chinex for base coat painting

b. Stipple brushes for distressing glazes in fine patterns

c. Inexpensive chip brushes for wall glazing and blending

d. Fine-haired, inexpensive, white China-bristle brushes for trim stries and antiquing with oil glazes

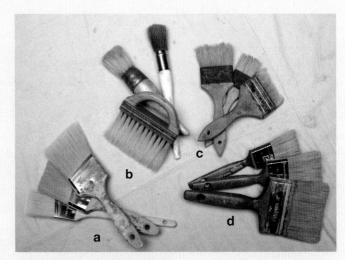

Brushes for large painting projects

BRUSH ALTERNATIVES

a. Bird feathers for marbleing (goose works best and can be notched for more versatility)

b. Steel and rubber combs for wood-graining and wall finishing

c. Sponges and baby rollers for base-coating sample boards (and some glazing techniques)

d. High-quality paper towels for glazing and cleaning up

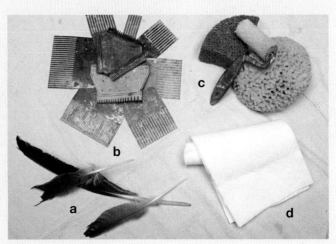

Brush alternatives

lay them out

Faux-painting projects that decorate beyond simple-process finishes call for a variety of layout tools. The following items were used in this book's projects:

a. Mechanical pencils with soft lead can be used to mark a surface. When used lightly, the lead is easily removable.

b. Soft gum erasers remove lead residue from painted surfaces without burnishing the surface. Never use a hard rubber eraser, which leaves burnished "ghosts" that are visible when the surface is viewed at an angle, such as walking down a hall.

c. Steel or wood rulers, squares, and straightedges

d. Lightweight, aluminum levels in a variety of sizes

e. Lightweight string for establishing long straight lines beyond the length of a 6-foot (1.8 m) straightedge

f. Permanent markers for registering stencils and marking batches of paint

g. Compasses for drawing circular motifs. The large compass describes arcs of several feet and is useful in particular for ceiling medallions.

h. Snap cutters and mat knifes are indispensable for stencil making, taping layouts, and all sorts of cleanup operations.

i. Taper knives and putty knives for preparation, cleaning up, forcing stencils into corners, and Venetian plaster applications

j. Five-in-one tool for cleaning rollers, scraping preparation, and a million other possibilities; a favorite pocket tool for many faux finishers

PAPER AND BOARDS

a. Mylar for making stencils

b. Tracing paper for stencil making and mural transfers

c. 6-ply railroad board (also called oak tag)

d. Soft board for cutting stencils

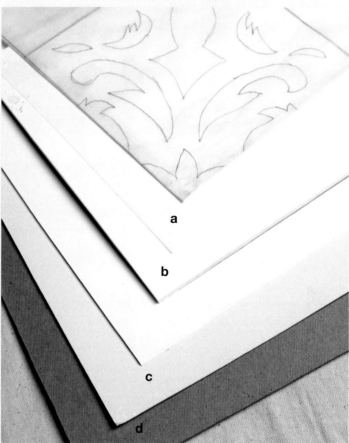

BE LIGHT WITH LEAD

Holding a pencil in the writing position always leaves a dark trail, which can ruin a project. Instead, use the grasp of a symphony conductor to leave an impression that should only be visible from close up, and can be removed with a soft gum eraser. Mechanical pencils with soft lead allow tight penciling against a ruler.

Stencils

Wallpaper evolved from stencils. French artisans who decorated Parisian interiors often rendered hand-painted walls in both scenic murals and patterns. Enterprising workers made an extra few francs by stenciling patterns on rectangles of paper called *dominoes*, which were mailed to rural customers who pasted them on the walls. Dominoes taped together became the first wallpaper roll. A velvetlike paper, *flock*, emerged when someone stenciled varnish instead of paint on the rolls, then dusted on fibers, which stuck to the varnish.

No one decorates quite like the French, and they elaborated the stencil idea to hand-cut woodblocks, which were inked and stamped on paper. Woodblock printing created simple patterned papers for the masses, and more expensive, scenic mural papers, which are essentially elaborate multicolored stencil jobs. Cheap French wallpapers flooded the market of the early years of the United States, ending the livelihoods of itinerant stencil artists whose work is now regularly exposed in historic restorations.

Historic wallpaper collections, such as the ones at Cooper-Hewitt National Design Museum in New York City and Sikkens Museum in Holland, offer great references for modern decorative painters who have revived custom stenciling.

Opaque materials, such as silk and oak tag, make old-fashioned stencil making a nightmare of pattern transfer and "blackening" with graphite. Modern stencilers lay transparent Mylar over a photocopied pattern and just "cut away."

This block-printed, scenic mural
wallpaper was made using methods
derived from stencil making.

MAKING STENCILS AT HOME

Precut stencils can be purchased from a wide range of suppliers, or they can be made at home, which is more time consuming but far more creatively rewarding. Most of the time required for any stencil project is taken up by pattern selection and cutting.

Much of the book information about stencil making is obsolete. Photocopy machine enlargements eliminate the laborious process of gridding up, or enlarging, patterns. Transparent plastics such as Mylar, now used for stencil making, eliminate the filthy, charcoal methods of pattern transfer that were used in the past.

When making stencils, use 4 or 5 mm–thick, frosted Mylar sheets, 24" × 36" (61 × 91.4 cm) in size, purchased at an art supply store. The frost-ing does not eliminate the transparency of the Mylar, but allows it to be written on with a pencil. Thinner Mylar and drafting vellum are too flimsy for stencil making, and tend to rip easily. These Mylars are suitable for smaller-border stencil making and one-use stencils.

To make the stencils, tape a photocopied pattern against a piece of Mylar. Allow some room for waste around the outside of the pattern. Later, when striking the stencil with paint, the waste border will prevent paint from being applied outside the pattern onto the wall. Cut the stencil against a soft, thick cardboard (not corrugated), using a snap knife. (Always retract the blade after use to keep your hands safe and the blade very sharp.)

masking and painter's tape

Avoid cheap masking tape: it damages surfaces and leaves glue residues, which darken over time. The extra money spent on better-quality tape will always be recouped.

Higher-quality, blue painter's tape comes in a range of quality, and is suitable for most projects. The more economical types are similar to masking tape, and work only for masking trim and floors. Despite the high cost, professionals prefer blue tape with an orange core or center ring because it will not tear paint off properly primed surfaces if removed carefully. Other useful tapes include wide paper masking with mastic on one edge, and narrow "car-striping tapes" which are low-tack and suitable for many decorating techniques.

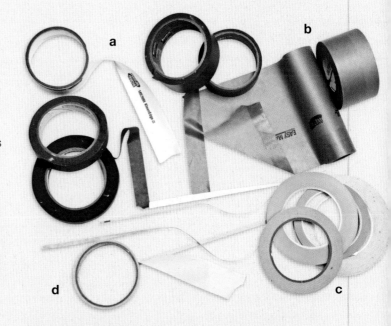

(a) The highest-quality blue tape has an orange core (unlike its imitators) and has general, multipurpose use. (b) Wide brown tapes have mastic on one side only. (c) Narrow "low grab" tapes are available at auto supply and art stores. (d) Masking tape has no place in the painter's tool box because of its damaging mastic.

decorating with paint

Preparing a wall for painting is like creating the canvas for a masterpiece; the best preparation bears the most attractive results. When fabrics and furniture are factored in as part of the scheme, interior decoration is created, not just another paint treatment. The painted embellishment of surfaces must be a part of, but not dominate, the space.

Choice of color is the most important element for the success of any finishing. Great color can carry mediocre finishing skills, but a poor color scheme is always a failure, regardless of the refined technique.

The finisher also must be aware of exposure to chemicals and protecting the dwelling against damage.

Top left: Factory-finished, worn switch plates and vents. Bottom right: Switch plates with a shellac primer faux treatment

Preparing a Room to Paint

Good housekeeping habits make for a good paint treatment, and will take the project further for a faux finish. Success demands a clear plan of action based on having a suitable sample of the finish; setting up the area for painting; good preparation; and the painting job itself. A major portion of the any painting project includes cleanup.

Prepare the space by masking off areas that need protection from paint spatters. Furniture and breakable items should be removed from the room or covered for protection. Always allow ample time for cleaning paint tools immediately after they are used.

Gather all materials, paints, and sundries in advance. Avoid losing time in costly trips to the hardware store for some overlooked item. Painting is a time-consuming, repetitive task best dispatched in substantial blocks of time without interruptions. Turn off the cell phone.

"Box in" furniture to the center of the work area, placing it in a compact, stable pile. Allow an ample, ladder-wide path around the perimeter of the room. Moving things once painting has begun results in paint-covered hands getting color in the wrong places. Cover consolidated furnishings with canvas drop cloths or plastic sheeting before sanding preparation. Remove furniture entirely from the room if the floors are to be finished. An empty room makes it easy to spot undesirable features before they dry. An empty room also allows for freedom of movement and a faster job in the end.

Unscrew all switch plates, vents, and electronic device covers from the surfaces to be painted, and put them in a bucket. These small items are easy to lose.

INTERIOR LIGHTING FOR PAINTING

It's important to light rooms properly before decorative painting. Many areas of a dwelling will be dark when the furniture lighting is removed. Construction sites often lack any lighting whatsoever. Large work lamps sold at home improvement centers offer the best option for supplemental lighting. However, they provide strong illumina-

decorating switch plates

Decorating switch plates to match wall and trim finishes is a nice way to carry the treatment further. Lightly sand the switchplates with a fine paper and place them on a piece of corrugated cardboard. Poke small holes in the cardboard with your screwdriver, and push the plate screws through to secure them. Spray with an aerosol can of white shellac in a well-ventilated area. The primed plates should receive the same base coats and faux finishing steps to blend nicely in the final décor.

This faux-finished switch plate almost disappears.

Above: Extra-smooth surfaces were prepared for Venetian plaster panels and surrounds, bordered with real gold-leaf detail on the moldings.

Left: Glasslike effects for wall glazing are obtained over an ultra-smooth ground. The preparation phase is more time consuming than the final painting steps.

tion that is very different than the finished room will have, and thus offer little help in considering the suitability of the finish from a decorative standpoint. Do not determine the faux finish for a room under the glare of work-lamp conditions.

Work lights generate a lot of heat and can easily create burns when carelessly handled. Be sure to restrict children's access to painting locations.

COVERING FLOORS

Before you begin, protect floors with a heavy canvas drop cloth made specifically for painters. Be advised: wood floors with glossy varnish or waxed finishes are extremely slippery under drops, opening the door for dangerous accidents. If people will be passing through the room during the refurbishing, drop cloths should be removed at the end of each work period.

It's also possible to protect wood and stone floors using heavy, red rosin construction paper, which comes in large rolls. Papering floors is suitable for jobs that need longer periods of work. When papering floors, cut and fit the paper and secure it with a high-quality painter's tape. Paper also works great in difficult-to-cover areas such as baths, around fixtures, and on kitchen countertops. Take care to not drop a lot of water on the paper, which can lead to the red dyes leaching. The dye can be absorbed by certain flooring materials, such as unsealed stone, causing stains that are sometimes impossible to remove. Wood floors that are slated for refinishing often receive no protection during painting work. Paint spatters will be sanded off.

Instead of papering over carpet, use cellophane made for that purpose, available at many carpeting suppliers. Cellophane carpet is then covered with canvas drop cloths.

The care spent protecting floors is rewarded doubly with savings in cleanup. It's wise to clean up paint on floors immediately with water or the correct solvent while it is still soft. Next-day dry paint might come off with water and vigorous scrubbing; if not, try a solvent. Scrubby pads or careful scraping with single-edge razor blades is the next course of action, but using these often dulls the sheen on varnished floors and could remove a sealer coat on stone.

Before painting the base moldings next to carpeting, place an inexpensive masking tape next to the wood and force it down toward the floor with a flat-edged, wide taping knife, which slightly compresses the carpet. Remove the tape after the painting steps are dry, and the carpet will spring back.

SEALING OFF OPEN AREAS

Overhead painting projects can create flying spatters, so tape or use pushpins to fasten inexpensive plastic above moldings, on cabinetry, and over stairway balusters. Plastic sheeting fixed over door openings will minimize the possibility of dust from heavy sanding jobs settling in other areas of the home.

Decorative plastering and texture painting are extremely sloppy. It's best to mask all trim work.

Surface Preparation

The time spent smoothing trim and walls consumes a large portion of any finishing project. The greater the sheen of the old paint finish, the more involved the preparation for the base coat. Don't count on faux finishes to conceal bad surfaces. A lack of prep work is likely to accentuate defects.

A bumpy, irregular ground will compromise the appearance of a glazed finish. Sanding with fine paper makes a tremendous improvement, and promotes adhesion of the paint layers.

Polished Venetian plasters can bring to light old, poorly patched picture hook holes and irregular corner taping. For plasterwork that will be polished, walls must be carefully patched, leveled, and sanded for a final smooth surface, which can then be polished to a glassy finish.

Gold leaf and metallic paints, like plasters, are reflective and unforgiving. Good prep and smoothing prior to decorating always pays dividends.

WALL PATCHING

Use joint compound for wall patching. Plan on applying three thin coats to level nail holes and voids. Walls that are slightly textured from previous paint rolling and sloppy applications can be skim coated—that is, troweled with a thin coat of compound over the entire surface, and then fine-sanded to provide a new, level surface. This is

Before and After: High-traffic areas especially need detailed preparation to guarantee that finishes will last. A good prep effort will reward with many years of durable decoration.

messy and time-consuming work. Skim coating is necessary for high-sheen finishes, and demands a complete coat of primer-sealer before proceeding.

TRIM PATCHING

Reserve vinyl spackle for trim work and floors, where a harder patch is in order. This kind of spackle demands more effort to sand smooth, making it a poor choice for walls.

When the spackle is dry, sand the patch with fine-grit paper. Abrasive sandpapers are numbered by the amount of sand particles per square inch; the higher the number, the smaller the size of the sand particles which determine the grit. Low-numbered, coarse papers such as 50 and 80 can leave scratches, and are used only for heavy paint removal. Scratches in the patch will show under sheen paint finishes. Do not use coarse grits for a final smoothing. Higher-numbered papers such as 150 and 220 are suitable for the final sanding before painting begins.

Finish each step of preparation before proceeding to the next. Patch, sand, and then clean up all dust with a vacuum before opening a can of paint. After vacuuming, spot-prime the patches; completely prime rooms that needed extensive repairs.

Safety from Exposure

Painting and finishing often involves exposure to hazards. Dust is the main source of problems during preparation. Solvent and chemical exposure is a concern while using the paints during the finishing process.

The paint workplace can also be a very dangerous place. Ladders and scaffolds, exposed electrical cords, and auxiliary lighting all present risks for accidents. Young children are especially attracted to the painting process, and might enter the work area when supervisors are not about.

DUST

Dust inevitably results from good surface preparation. Vinyl spackles—used for nail holes and voids in trim work—and drywall compounds that are popular for wall leveling both generate very fine dust when dry-sanded. Airborne dust from preparation easily finds its way throughout a house,

sandpaper tells a story

If you're not sure what kind of paint exists on walls or trim to be refinished, test it by sanding the surface with a fine sandpaper in an inconspicuous spot. A crisp sound, which leaves fine dust on the paper, indicates oil paint; a dull sound with the paper sliding over the surface and no dust indicates latex. Remember the cardinal rule of painting: use oil over water, but not water over oil.

Wax is sometimes found on furniture, stained trim, and floors. Sandpaper slides on a wax surface, clogging the paper with black gum. Wax must be completely removed with mineral spirits and steel wool. It's a very discouraging process, but absolutely necessary for new paint to "stick" to the surface.

Left to right: Wax clogs fine paper with black gum; latex is sanded off the surface in rubbery chunks; old oil paint sands to powder.

Protective gear, left to right: powdered, vinyl disposable gloves; cloth dust mask; zip-top storage bag; cartridge respirator

especially with forced-air heating systems. You can minimize dust circulation by placing fans in windows to direct dust toward the outside.

Fine "prep" dust irritates the lungs and skin. Protect yourself with the use of surgical-style dust masks. Cover as much of your body as possible with a long-sleeved shirt and a hat. Sanded areas should be brushed down and vacuumed immediately after prep work is completed. This keeps dust from spreading further, and contributes to a healthy work zone. Lingering dust also reduces the quality of a finish.

THE FLAVOR OF LEAD

Lead dust, bewilderingly, has a very agreeable taste and odor, like almonds. A widely publicized health hazard occurs when children eat the paint chips in older homes because they taste good.

LEAD

Lead was a common component of most oil-based paints before laws eliminated it in the 1950s. Old-timer painters suffered debilitating health conditions, such as fatigue and cartilage degeneration, from constant exposure to lead. Be aware that lead is present in the sanding dust of older buildings. Vacuuming dust and preventing its circulation to other areas of the building are doubly important when working around lead. Many municipalities have health regulations concerning lead. You can test for lead with inexpensive kits that are widely available at home centers.

FUMES

Treat manufacturers' claims of green technology with skepticism. Solvent exposure is still a concern, despite great strides in removing them from paints. Many newer water-base products contain chemical ingredients that have not been fully tested. Ammonia is common in many water-base house paints, and the hazards from long-term exposure to it remain unknown.

The odor of paints is not a reliable indicator of a hazard. One of the most toxic solvents in painting is benzene (now seldom used), which is odorless. Some paints smell fine because perfumes have been added to offset disagreeable odors. This does not make the chemicals in the paints any safer.

Avoid using petroleum-solvent, oil-base paints as much as possible to minimize exposure. Yet some finishing techniques and primers that convert oil-base grounds to latex involve oil solvents.

Cloth sanding masks are not capable of protecting against chemical vapors; it's best to use respirator masks to filter vapors out of the air. Respirators have charcoal cartridges, which remove most solvents from the air stream. The masks are uncomfortable to wear but necessary where breathing conditions are tight. Fit the respirator tight to the face, following directions, and keep the mask stored in a zip-top bag when not in use. This keeps the charcoal filter fresh for further use. Solvent vapors also pass through the skin, so keep the body covered as much as possible with a long, sleeved shirts and pants.

The flow of fresh air to an area remains the best method to control solvent exposure. A large floor fan exchanges the air in a room in a few minutes. Even when working with so-called safe paints, a good air exchange keeps your work zone comfortable by removing excessive water vapor and odors.

Paints are colored with pigments, which often contain toxic metals, such as cadmium for yellow colors. Wash your hands frequently, especially around eating time and after work is completed for the day.

Gloves offer extra protection. Thin, cotton garden gloves work fine when holding paintbrushes and rollers. Use powdered vinyl and latex disposable gloves for more hands-in-the-paint activities such as wall glazing. Buy the gloves in bulk; boxes are modestly priced at hardware stores or medical supply houses. Latex gloves are not resistant to solvents, and can cause allergic reactions in some people. Powdered vinyl is the most popular among professional finishers.

disposing of paints and solvents

Save modest amounts of paint mixed for the job in small, airtight containers for future touchups. Containers from the recycling bin or small, vinyl, screw-cap jars from an art store are excellent. Label all the materials carefully. This way, touchups can be done years in the future, when the memory of formulas and ratios has long faded.

When disposing of paints and solvents, never pour them down a drain or directly into the environment. Leave unwanted latex and other water-based products in open containers. When the material has dried up, it can be disposed of in regular household garbage. Keep solvents and oil-base paints labeled in tight containers, preferably their original ones. Dispose of them on hazardous-waste collection days offered by many municipalities.

Treat oily rags, especially from oil-based glazing work, with respect. A small quantity bundled tightly (such as in a plastic bag) can spontaneously ignite, leading to a fire. Rag fires have burned just-painted houses to the ground. Pour water over discarded rags and wrap them in plastic, or stuff them into an empty paint can so they do not dry out, and include them with your solid waste.

Many municipalities sponsor hazardous waste collection days. Check local news media for details. Latex paints, especially off-whites, are boxed together by the collectors and distributed to contractors for reuse—a heartening fact.

A World of Color

For sophisticated decorating results, use store-mixed "custom" colors along with paint manufacturers' recommended color combinations. The best look often demands colors to be handmixed on site for a particular scheme. Experienced painters and decorators might start with a "mother-color" close to the desired scheme, and make small alterations to that color to achieve the desired finish. Many painters learn the practical methods of altering batches of colors for great results without ever opening a book on color theory.

The extensive literature on color theory confuses painters by the use of abstract concepts. Ideas about colors—such as which ones please versus those that do not—are often derived from cultural differences and style. Commonly cited rules—such as "cool colors recede," "warm colors advance," and "moods are elicited by particular colors"—are mastered only with years of experience.

The popularity of colors changes over the decades. The lemon yellow smeared everywhere in the 1960s is absent today, whereas its fellow traveler, avocado green, fell out of favor only to return recently under a new name. Green remains the most popular color for interior schemes, but a sage green or olive appears contemporary, whereas aqua greens dominated the 1990s.

To acquire a feel for classic, contemporary, or other desirable color combinations, study the extensive selections of rooms pictured in interior design books and magazines, and the photo gal-

TINTED CEILING

When painting a room with a strong color or faux finish, add a touch of the color to the ceiling batch to tint it in the direction of the finish (as long as everything else does not match). This light value on the ceiling creates intimacy with a more unified color look, and helps accentuate crown-molding treatments through contrast.

Finished ceilings with a tinted paint formula or a faux finish technique are an important touch. This dining room was base-coated with a gold metallic, then glazed with a transparent bronze.

leries in these pages. Tear out inspiring, attractive pages, and create a file of favorites to help visualize choices. Selections made on impulse offer valuable direction; this can be thought of as feeling color, not thinking it.

Older books from the library illustrate how soon many colors become dated; this cautions against the use of strict formulas and reinforces the necessity of observation and intuition, two elements that are often ignored.

A few guidelines are helpful; use the following when making color choices and planning combinations.

Warm colors greatly predominate over cool in decorating choices made by professional decorators and interior designers. A common example of this idea is linen white, which is warmed by a touch of yellow for painting trim work. The cool choice for trim would be a pure white, which is antiseptic, as the decorator might say. The majority of off-whites offered on paint charts are in the warm family. An example of a warm choice for a darker color is brick red, which is warmed by some yellow, versus some burgundies which can become cool under the influence of magenta. Many paint companies have information on the paint strips that key their custom colors as being warm or cool.

Value is the amount of lightness and darkness of a color. Baby blue and navy are extreme examples of a light and dark value of blue. Always start with the lighter value of two selections when choosing from a store-supplied paint strip. It's a common decorating error to choose too dark a value when judging small strips.

A too-dark batch of paint is often saved by adding equal amounts of white to lighten it. More white can be added as taste demands. Remember that pure white tends to cool a color, so tinting a batch with a warm off-white such as linen will keep the batch warm. You can also darken values by adding raw umber in small amounts to create shades. Black can be used for shades, but its harshness makes it an unpopular choice with most colorists.

Beware of the use of monochromatic color schemes, such as a group of tints all taken from the same mother color (or the same paint strip).

This idea works great for fashion in matching elements of an outfit, but produces a commercial look when used in decorating homes.

Novice home stylists often match paint colors to furniture fabrics and window treatments. Go for *a mix, not a match,* of colors for sophisticated decorating, and you'll save a great deal of misspent energy making small adjustments to colors. Fabrics are made with dyes; paint with pigments matches of these elements will change as the light in a room shifts with the time of day and season. A perfectly color-matched room is mediocre decorating at best.

Hue answers the question, "What color is it?" Red, blue, and yellow are the primary hues of color that comprise the color wheel. The primary hues are mixed to create the secondary hues of orange (red mixed with yellow), green (yellow and blue), and violet (red and blue).

A key concept for interior design is the use of complementary colors in some form. Complementary colors sit opposite each other on the color wheel. Red is the theoretical complement of green; blue, of orange; and yellow, of violet. This concept provides the framework for mixing a variety of colors for paints, or for selecting fabrics and wall finishes in a room. Complementary schemes create the most spectacular results.

Mixing pastels with their complements creates a pleasing gray. For example, add a small amount of a strong red to a sizable quantity of white to create a soft pink. Add the complementary green into the pink, slowly softening it to a neutral gray. Use that gray tone to color a glaze over the pink ground, or tint the gray to an off-white, and use it as a trim color with pink walls.

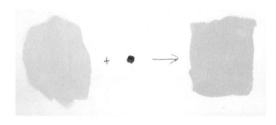

A gray tone is mixed from a pink one by adding green, the complement. This approach reliably produces an interesting combination.

neutralize brights with complementary colors

Experiment with mixing complementary colors. It won't change the value—making a color lighter or darker—but instead will change the hue. A too-vibrant red batch can be softened by the addition of small amounts of green. Increasing the amount of green would take the red into a neutral, gray range of extremely interesting selections. Likewise, a too-green hue can be softened to olive by the addition of red. Complementary mixed grays are not the dead grays made by adding black to white. Like all mixes, a complementary combination can be tinted with white or shaded with raw umber.

Red fabrics visually mix with drab, olive paint effects for a complementary color scheme.

Use white plus one: Any color—vibrant, deep-tone, or pastel—will partner well with whites that are slightly warmed with the addition of yellows. A striking wall color with an off-white trim is a time-tested decorating formula.

Neutral colors as textures produce restful and quiet surroundings. Faux textures such as weaves and stries perform well in these color departments.

Consider historical color combinations. Create Southwest and Tuscan styles with an earthy palette of yellow ochre, siennas, and umbers. Swedish style is a palette of blue mixed with its complement to almost gray, and warm or cool off-whites.

Making Samples for the Space

Having an adequate and accurate sample in hand before the first piece of furniture is moved helps to guarantee a successful project. It is not uncommon to produce a dozen samples before painting begins.

When redecorating, spend some time evaluating the contents that will accent the finishing. Consider fabric colors and textures, carpeting, furniture, and the floor's wood tones in the color scheme. Changes to these elements, and other aspects such as new window treatments or carpentry alterations, are important decisions to be made in advance.

New houses, additions, and extensive remodels are challenging to visualize because there is no "before" stage. Try to assemble the elements as best you can from material swatches, stained wood samples, and manufacturers' catalog pictures.

SAMPLE PORTABILITY

Samples should not be made on the walls in the room until you are very sure of your choice and need a final check. Besides making a mess in a room not ready for painting, a lengthy sample-making process will result in a multitude of color swatches on the wall; a confusing patchwork quilt of ideas.

It's better to make all the samples on boards that can be easily moved about to help judge variations in light, which are often dramatic in a room. Moreover, boards are portable and can be

Mix a few drops of green into a vibrant red to quiet it down.

MIXING METHODS

It's easy to alter a batch of color by adding small increments of tinting pigments (universal colors) or larger amounts of a premixed paint. When using two different colors on a project, try mixing them in various ratios. Without knowing any color theory, this approach produces a great amount of successful choices.

Mix complimentary colors in small quantities, such as red with green, will create less saturated options. Tint those options with varying quantities of white to create a plethora of options for a color scheme.

mix vs. match

Mahogany furniture has color hues resolutely in the red family. The match would be a strong red wall finish, or a red tinted with white, yielding pink. However, deep red would be acceptable but hardly spectacular, and a pink match, especially in a dining room, would set up a disagreeable vibration.

A mix would be better for this decorating scheme: a drab olive in a deeper value, or a sage green in the light range. Both of these green family members are complements of red, and each softens red's vibrancy. Green decorative elements, such as fabrics, provide a soothing mix in any scheme that is predominately red.

Viewing a wealth of samples informs the faux-finishing process.

taken to places such as carpet centers to help make choices in the decorating process. Bear in mind that because they are made by hand, faux finishes always differ to a degree from the sample to the job.

For wall treatments, choose acid-free boards such as railroad board or mat board, sold at most art stores. These will accept water-base paints without wrinkling. They can be affixed to walls with tape secured on their reverse sides, then saved for consideration in other projects. Rigid foam core is another popular board for sample making, but is more expensive and bulky if one is building a collection.

Pieces of wood trim are perfect for millwork samples such as doors, cabinetry, and crown moldings. Be aware that plastic, extruded moldings are increasingly substituted for wood detailing, and take a finish differently than wood elements. Always make samples on materials that replicate the existing conditions as closely as possible. For a

process that involves stained wood as the first step, make the samples on blanks of the actual wood. Cherry wood is a very different ground than similarly colored mahogany.

Construction projects are excellent sources of scraps, often available for free from piles of discarded material—or you can arrange to obtain scraps from a builder.

LABELING SAMPLES

As a sample takes shape, note each step on the back. Notes made separately on paper tend to get lost, and memory is a poor guide, especially when the sample-making process produces a large selection. On the actual sample, leave a small portion of each step of the finish exposed for easy duplication. Even experts can be challenged to determine a base coat buried under a few steps of glazing. It's wise to make an additional small sample during the project, carefully labeled and saved as a valuable record for future touch-ups.

Paint samples for rooms that enjoy mostly evening traffic, such as this dining room, should be created with artificial, not natural light in mind.

Light the Way

The light source is the most important factor for correctly choosing a faux finish. Most people fail to consider it. A textured stone finish can seem theatrical if there is too much contrast in its elements when viewed in daylight. Considered under the dim illumination of a cellar, it will soften to realistically imitate cave walls. Because of the lighting, a finish must, if possible, always be evaluated in the area where it will be used.

NATURAL LIGHT

Fine artists, such as the French impressionist Claude Monet, have spent lifetimes recording the nuances of natural lighting. Normal, daylight sun is the hardest to consider, because it varies in brightness over the course of the day, as well as through the season. Also, tropical and temperate daylights are different creatures. Color that is too saturated and vibrant for northern climes is softened to pastel under equatorial daylight.

VIEWING SAMPLE BOARDS

Try to complete and view proposed samples in the actual room before setting up for painting. A room stripped of all its elements, with a mountain of white canvas drop cloths in place, makes for skewed color consideration.

Always view samples at a distance—say, six to eight feet (1.8 to 2.4 m)—to see how they will look in the finished room. Do not hold the sample at arm's length, but place it against a wall and step back some distance. Try to view it under the actual finished lighting conditions, if possible.

Interior designers also consider the difference in direct sunlight flooding into windows, and northern light—diffused daylight reflected into windows from all directions on the outside. A north-facing room on a house will always show a color differently from the south side.

ARTIFICIAL LIGHT

Artificial light comes from electrical fixtures: incandescent, florescent, and halogen. Light from fireplaces and candles, also considered artificial, are factors in interior design as well. Incandescent light from the classic light bulb—still the most prevalent type of interior residential lighting—casts a soft yellowish light which bathes everything in a warm glow.

Fluorescent fixtures predominate in commercial setting, but are less a factor in residential settings. They alter the perception of color tremendously. Designers favor neutral colors in commercial spaces to avoid this problem.

Halogen lights are close to daylight, and greatly favored these days in fixed lighting in residential interiors. Halogen light is harsh. Recessed halogens in ceilings tend to place the viewer at an angle to the surface, which accentuates every minor flaw in wall and trim surfaces. For this reason, steer clear of high-sheen finishes such as polished plaster where ceiling halogens provide illumination.

Be sure to consider the limitations of daylight in making decorating choices. The time of day a room is used is an important factor. Dining rooms and bedrooms are night rooms and deserve consideration under artificial lighting. A pinkish red becomes rich burgundy under nighttime lights. Carpets and furniture that are matched and mixed to a faux finish in a home decorating center under fluorescent fixtures might yield unpleasant color surprises when the pieces take their positions in a finished room.

Mixing Paints and Matching Samples

Color matching and replication of paint mixes are valued skills in faux finishing. To avoid creating great quantities of difficult-to-dispose waste, make samples with small amounts of paint and glaze.

You'll save money; the cost of material in rejected mixtures canbe considerable.

When a sample is chosen, you will need to match the recipe in a large quantity. Being able to reliably recreate a finish is a rule of good faux finishing. A single batch of the large amount needed for a room-size project can be mixed at once—or a system for measuring calibrated quantities can be employed. This matches the original batch as the need arises, and avoids a large amount of waste. Making paint recipes without noting the measurements of quantities can make duplication later aggravating and even impossible.

MIXING BASE COATS AND GLAZES

When producing samples for an opaque paint formula, paint small swatches on scraps of railroad board in a thick manner. When dry, these paint swatches can be taken to most paint stores where a computer can match the color. The samples must be thickly applied for the computer to read them successfully. When formulated by the computer, the color can be reproduced dependably in any volume and in any sheen, such as gloss or satin.

Saved color swatches are helpful for smaller batches of paint, which are duplicated by hand mixing. Whenever a color is altered by adding small amounts of another color, record each step on a sample strip of board, with handwritten notes indicating the additional color added and the approximate amount. When attempting to remix the color, first make a small batch and when it dries, compare it to the original sample. Remember that colors darken as they dry, so comparisons are always made wet-to-wet or dry-to-dry.

An inventory of many color swatches and sample boards can be confusing. Careful note-taking keeps everything clear.

THE ALL-IMPORTANT GLAZE-TO-PAINT RATIO

Making samples and duplicating an acceptable sample for a large project involve careful measurements of glaze-to-paint proportions. The glazing concoction is made by adding paint to glazing liquid. With sufficient paint on hand, larger batches of glaze concoctions may be mixed as the need arises simply by calibrating the glaze-to-paint proportion. Measure carefully to avoid wasting expensive materials and the headache of disposing unused paint products.

The ratio of glaze to paint is variable, depending on the desired result. For antiquing projects, such as cabinetry with the country look, glaze is mixed with paint in small quantities, such as one part glaze to three parts paint (1:3). The concoction is brushed on, creating an almost opaque coverage, but allows the base coat to peek through on edges and moldings. For wall techniques, such as suedes and stones, a concoction might call for two parts glaze to one part paint (2:1). A higher proportion of glazing liquid increases the transparency, making for soft, subtle effects. Proportions as great as 20:1 serve well for wall weaves and stries on trim work. Use careful calibration when measuring such disparate proportions.

Strie or dragged finishes work well when decorating trims of cabinetry.

ensuring paint matches

Not all store-mixed paint will match from can to can. When remixing a batch, take care to duplicate the original batch.

To ensure the match, place a clean mixing paddle in one container, and then dip it half as deep into a second container. A strong line between the formulas indicates a mismatch. This wet-on-wet matching avoids the additional time needed to dry paints, which for oil paints can be hours.

COLOR FORMULA (left to right):
linen white (base coat), beige
(glaze)

COLOR-WASHING

Calibrate a glazing concoction made of one part midtone eggshell latex paint with three parts quality acrylic glazing liquid, and then decorate a wall with sponges and paper towels. This workhorse of a technique is the basic building block, and can be elaborated into marbles, clouds, and other faux finishes.

MATERIALS

water-base eggshell paint: linen white (base coat),
midtone khaki beige (for coloring glaze)
glazing liquid (with long open time)

TOOLS

basic layout and painting tools (see page 26)

orange core tape, 1½" (3.8 cm) wide

fist-size natural sea sponge

3" (7.6 cm) chip brush or fan brush

paint trays

high-quality paper towels

INSTRUCTIONS

1. Wet the sponge and wring out until it is damp. Dip the sponge lightly in the glaze, and tap the excess against the cardboard.

2. Starting in an upper corner of the room, sponge the glaze in an irregular shape in an area that covers approximately 2 square feet (0.2 sq m). If too large an area is covered with each application, the paint will dry too quickly, and there will not be enough open time to distress the glaze.

3. Feather some of the sponged-on glaze into the corner and along the ceiling line with the chip brush. Novices tend to load too much glaze into the corners and edges along moldings, which dries darker than the rest of the finish and looks disagreeable.

VARIATION

Create a sample strip of a color combination by calibrating different proportions of the color with glaze. Try 1 part paint to 6 parts glaze, and then twelve parts glaze, which doubles the transparency with the subsequent sample.

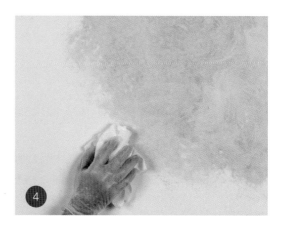

4. Crumple a paper towel into a wad and soften the glaze into a cloud. Rotate the hand as you work, distressing it so it is "evenly uneven."

5. Repeat the glaze application in an adjacent area, leaving a small gap between the already-worked areas. Do not overlap glaze applications, as dark lines called *lapmarks* will develop in the finish.

6. Distress the open glaze, carefully pushing it into the gap between applications. If desired, the same or another glaze can be applied on subsequent days to create a multiple-glaze color-washing.

PRACTICE MAKES PERFECT

This color-washing process is easily mastered with a bit of practice. Plunge in, do a wall, make a mess, and then repaint it. The second time around will show tremendous improvement. Putting the hand to the paint is the most important step.

calibrate a small concoction

Measure small quantities of paints and glaze with plastic spoons for making samples. Fill the spoon and level it with a straight-edged putty knife for a single measurement. Empty the contents into a clean mixing cup. Use a small brush to wipe the spoon contents into the cup. Repeat for additional measurements. In the same manner, mix one unit of satin house paint with three units of transparent glaze, creating a concoction with a 1:3 ratio. This ratio is fairly common for a standard wall-glazing job. Create a simple color-wash, strie, and combed sample on the same ground-glazing concoction.

A mother color–to–glaze concoction can be distressed with several techniques. Note the different values each technique creates with the same glaze transparency. For trim to be glazed in a strie, and for a match with color-washed walls, different transparencies of the same mother-color are necessary because of the effect of the tool and the weight of the hand.

To sample for transparency, fill a small plastic cup with the 1:3 mixture and label it with a marker. Pour half the amount into a second cup, and add an equal amount of glaze. Pour half of that and save the rest, labeled, to the side. Repeat again. The results are three small batches with glaze-to-paint ratios of approximately 1:3, 1:6, and 1:12. A fourth batch,1:18, was made by adding one-third more glaze to the 1:12 batch. With the concoctions made, proceed to making samples and evaluate them when dry.

After a successful sampling, prepare to mix a room-size batch. Measure the units in small plastic cups. As the batch is depleted, repeat the calibration process. Only a small amount of material should remain at the end of a project, which is stored in a tight container for future touch-ups.

BASIC MEASUREMENTS

A rule of thumb for making wall-size glaze quantities: Mix the glaze-paint concoction with half the amount of base coat used for painting. A room that needed 1 gallon (3.8 L) for the base coat can be comfortably glazed with ½ gallon (945 ml) of mixture.

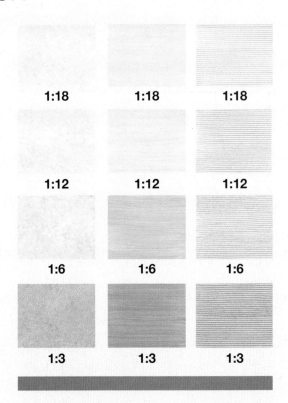

A midtone apricot mother color is mixed with different proportions of glazing liquid in measured calibrations. The samples increase in opacity from the top left to the bottom right. Each column of samples is distressed with a different technique: (left to right) color wash, strie, and comb. The paint-to-glaze ratio is documented beneath each swatch, so the exact batch can be duplicated.

MATERIALS

water-base eggshell paints:
linen white (base coat), midtone beige
(glaze color)
water-base glazing liquid (fast-drying)

TOOLS

basic layout and painting tools (see page 26)
sea sponge
strie brushes
steel combs
paper towels
small plastic cups

A handful of colors mixed in different transparencies created this complex faux marble panel. Expert understanding of marble and painstaking layout during the project's execution makes this trompe l'oeil deception particularly convincing.

single-step faux finishes

It's easy to create impressive decorating style with single-process, glaze-and-paint techniques. Broken-color effects with attractive names such as *suedeing* and *pebbling* can complement any interior scheme. All that's required are careful color consideration and a low-contrast combination.

Left: Sponging decorates these walls in pebbled soft olive tones. See the Technique Tutorial, Sponging On, page 63.

Right: Color-washed walls create a relaxing effect with natural, textured fabrics.

Right: A transparent gray glaze was stippled diffusely over a platinum metallic base coat in a simple square motif, imitating silver leaf. The walls were hand-trowled with green Venetian plaster, the arches and bases were hand-painted with a dramatic marble effect, and a few coats of gloss varnish were added.

Facing page: A midtone beige glaze over an off-white ground produced the soft mottling inside the wall panels, which were further embellished with painted a trellis, florals, and gold-leafed moldings. Soft, green rag work between the panels provides a foil for the busy detailing and murals on the first level.

Below: Cabinetry glazed in a low-contrast strie benefits from a second pass over some of the moldings for detail. High-traffic items need several clear finish coats for durability. See the single-step Technique Tutorial, Strie On Trim, page 64.

This room uses very dark, saturated colors made into glazes that are ragged and dragged over light grounds. Moorish patterns on the muraled closet doors evoke North African–inspired style.

Burnt orange crackle medium creates texture on these walls. A brown glaze was color-washed over the crackled surface, evoking a suede effect.

This room first received a bright gold metallic paint base. Various glaze transparencies were mother-colored with bronze and copper, and mica metallics were intermixed. Stipple, rag, and marble processes were used to make the faux finish.

Torn tissue paper is applied with wallpaper adhesive and allowed to dry. First base-coated with a platinum metallic paint, the walls were then glazed with gold metallic to highlight the folds in the paper. A beige-tone glaze stippled on the bathtub surround was then wiped off the highest reaches of the scrolled moldings for a worn look. Both glaze processes expertly highlight textured grounds.

Ultrasoft stipple finishes on lime and cordovan grounds gives a hint of texture, and thus interest, to strong colors that seem unfinished when solid. This type of wall glazing suits a modern décor in which patterning is best displayed, either minimally or maximally (such as in the carpets and fireplace here), but not in between. See the single-step Technique Tutorial, The Stippled Look, page 66.

Above: This master bedroom is finished with a group of color-wash glaze combinations. Suede finishing on the cornice is simply a brown dark-toned glaze over a darker-toned base coat, softly rag-distressed for the appearance of texture. A metallic base coat in the crown and ceiling coffers is similarly distressed with a brown formulation.

Right: A midtone blue glaze on a light-value gray ground decorates this dresser. Steel combs were used to distress the glaze, which was stried on the small dividers between the drawers. Two coats of acrylic satin varnish protect paint-finished furniture. See the single-step Technique Tutorial, Combing Wet Glazes, page 65.

A soft, allover stipple finish is achieved with the greatest of effort because glazes dry quickly, and lap marks are then impossible to avoid. A midtone reddish-gray colored the glaze, decorating the background for this Renaissance painting. The moldings were stippled, then wiped of glaze, to expose the white base coat.

Color-washed walls feature a hand-painted tree; similar transparent mediums were used for the bird, leaves, and bark. Glaze for both the wall background and the detail painting create unity between the two elements.

Glazes mixed with house paints rendered all the elements in this garden-themed decoration.

■ PROFILE

Sigmund Aarseth, NORWAY

Michelangelo laid the groundwork for the Baroque style in late fifteenth- and early sixteenth-century Italy. The Sistine Chapel stands as his shining example. As Baroque-style painting spread throughout Europe, regional expressions of the style, tempered by local historical and aesthetic sensibilities, flourished.

In fact, Baroque's distinguishing curved lines are called *flourishes*, feature gilt surfaces and elaborate color selections. Rococo, even more ornate than Baroque, emerged in the early eighteenth century.

In remote reaches of Europe, a naïve Baroque style of elaborate floral embellishment and abstract marbleizing proliferated, identified today as folk painting. Rosemaling is the Norwegian version, and it flourished in rural outposts. Isolated districts developed distinct styles of rosemaling; antique

work is often traced to individuals by the particulars of the brushwork, much as handwriting identifies a person. Poor, rural Scandinavian immigrants carried their few pieces of treasured painted furniture to North America, where their influence survives and thrives as country-style painting.

Sigmund Aarseth is one of the living masters of the rosemaling style. As a young housepainter, he sought a higher level of skill by learning the traditional craft he saw around him. Aarseth took to scrolling brushes and instruction from the *maester-maler* Gunnar Nordbo, in the distinctive technique called *telemark*.

Aarseth credits many Japanese artisans as being some of the best contemporary rosemalers, readily marrying Asian brush painting to scrolling technique. This style is called *toyama telemark*.

Facing page: An exuberant, polychromatic palette details equally bright surfaces. Color-washed paneling receives the *maestermaler's* touch with hand-painted swags, which are rendered freely without guides or stencils. The work is finished with a variety of scrollers, flats, and other brushes.

Left: This door features a multicolored floral in a naïve Baroque style on its top panel, with a monochrome mural of various blue transparencies below. All work was rendered freehand.

Below: A complementary color scheme of grayed green against vibrant red cheers people who endure long winters with little sun. The marbleized panels on the ceiling and below the chair rail fit the painted décor perfectly, despite their deliberate naïve execution.

single-step faux-finishing techniques

As the name implies, single-step finishes require one layer of application. The following basic techniques—sponge, strie, combing, stippling, and french brush—are deceptively simple, but as a painter's skill increases, a wide spectrum of results can be created. The colors selected, the transparency of the glazing concoction, and the weight of the hand on the tool all combine for the final result.

THE HONORABLE SPONGE

Natural sea sponges and, more recently, synthetic sponges, enjoy a place of honor in the decoration of architectural surfaces in many parts of the world and throughout history.

The art of Ancient Crete shows examples of sponge decoration. The Scotch-Boardman house, a seventeenth-century Colonial-era edifice in Massachusetts, featured interior sponge decoration in charcoal gray over an almost-black hue. After World War II, England experienced a sponging craze on interior walls, fueled by a lack of wallpaper when resources were diverted for wartime manufacturing.

Sponge painting exploded onto the decorative scene in the mid-1980s. Straight sponging now sounds a bit passé, given the proliferation of unfortunate color combinations and amateur techniques. (The neighbor who takes a one-hour

sponging course at the local hardware store is guilty of such damage, and service station restrooms made over on a budget drive the point home.) In the hand of a skilled practitioner who has a fine-tuned eye for color choices, the sponge will yield décor that ranges from elegant to whimsical, with a durability and ease of maintenance unsurpassed in painted finishes.

The secrets for sponge success: always choose low-contrast, sophisticated color combinations, and use extreme attention to detail when finishing corners and areas abutting moldings. "Evenly uneven" is the goal.

The sponge remains an important tool for quickly building up areas of broken color. These can stand alone as wall finishes, or can be worked over with striping or stencil techniques to complete the "faux" look. Sponges can do double-duty as paint applicators for stencil techniques and marbleizing.

The type of sponge controls the finish, so choose carefully. For walls, a subtle pebble finish can be obtained from natural sea sponges. Live sea sponges have a pimply side, from which water is expelled. When used for paint application, this surface creates a stipplelike effect. If a large sponge is wet, then frozen, it can be cut through the middle with a serrated knife, exposing a surface that applies paint in small, broken fragments. Both effects create delicious surface detail. Experiment with different species of sponges to find ones that yield pleasing patterns. When selecting natural sponges for paint work, beware of those filled with sand—or more dangerously, glass spicules—which can seriously lacerate your hands.

COLOR FORMULA (left to right): olive green (base coat), olive green tint (sponge color)

SPONGING ON

Undiluted, water-base paint is suitable as the medium for this type of finishing. The base coat and sponge coat should have the same sheen, and should create low contrast to maximize softness. Higher-quality paints offer maximum durability and ease of touch-up. Avoid sponging on multiple colors, which tends to become too busy visually.

To prepare: Paint the walls with a midtone color. Afterward, tint the remaining paint with 1 part white to 3 parts base color to create a monochromatic color scheme. Paint sample boards to determine if a subtle contrast is made; if not, adjust the proportions slightly. The color will be difficult to see as it is sponged on, so pay close attention. This is not mindless application. The sponge color will dry slightly darker, creating a soft, pebbled surface. An example of this technique is shown on page 50.

MATERIALS

water-base matte paint: olive green (base coat), olive green tint (sponge color)

TOOLS

basic layout and painting tools (see page 26)

fist-size natural sea sponge

paint trays

INSTRUCTIONS

1. Dampen a natural sea sponge, and squeeze to almost dry.

2. Dip the sponge lightly in paint, making sure it is not overloaded to dripping. Dab the sponge on a piece of cardboard to remove excess paint.

3. Dab the loaded sponge on the painting surface, working from the corners in and from the top of walls to the bottom.

4. To ensure an evenly uneven result, rotate your wrist, blotting and pouncing the sponge as you dab. Do not press the sponge too hard to the surface, as this will result in drips and runs.

SPONGE SECRETS

Small, torn-up pieces of sponge are useful for starting corners and reaching difficult areas. Gather a cardboard box and a plastic food container for the sponging setup (which can also be used for most painting techniques in this book). Load the container modestly to avoid dunking the sponge and minimizing paint spills if the setup is overturned accidentally. With the sponge lightly loaded, dab it on the cardboard box before proceeding to the wall. Like paint roller trays, this set up fits nicely on the ladder tray-support, making it easy to use in lofty areas of rooms.

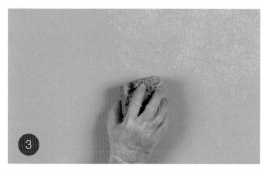

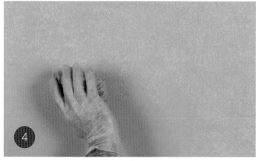

VARIATIONS

• A gloss, latex varnish can be sponged over any flat paint to create a sparkling effect, which works well with visually busy elements such as marble baths.

• Add tiny amounts of metallic paints to the varnish in approximately a 1:25 ratio for added sparkle.

VARIATIONS

• Old, funky brushes or expensive specialty brushes are useful for creating different variations in strie effects. For simple dragging on walls, work from top to bottom, completing an approximately 18" (45.7 cm) -wide section before starting the next. Work quickly, using large 4" to 6" (10.2 to 15.2 cm) –wide brushes for the application.

• Allow the first strie application to dry completely. The next day, repeat step 1 (with the same glaze), applying it in the cross direction to create a linen effect.

STRIE ON TRIM

Create linear patterns of strie (or "dragging") by brushing on transparent glazes, then distressing them with brushes or other tools. Oil-base formulas work best because their longer open time allows sufficient opportunity to create the desired effect, and oil-base concoctions set shortly after drying, which facilitates clear finishing with varnish or additional multiprocess steps.

For the glaze concoction, mix a midtone oil paint with 4 parts commercial glazing liquid and 2 parts mineral spirits. Mix thoroughly, as these components do not readily combine. An example of this technique is shown below and on page 52.

MATERIALS

water-base paint: latex eggshell (base coat)

oilbase paint: satin enamel (for glaze concoction)

mineral spirits

oil-base glazing liquid

TOOLS

basic layout and painting tools (see page 26)

China-bristle brushes, various sizes

steel combs

paper towels

INSTRUCTIONS

1. Load a fine-haired bristle brush with the glaze concoction, but do not overload it so it is dripping.

2. Paint the glaze on the moldings in the direction of the grain, keeping the application uniform. Do not paint a heavy layer in an attempt to make the material "cover." The ground should show through the glaze.

3. Once a section has been glazed, drag the glaze-depleted brush through the wet glaze on the molding. With uniform brush pressure, work from the corners out, and work quickly before the glaze begins to set—that is, lose its *open time*.

COMBING WET GLAZES

Combing wet glazes creates fabriclike effects for walls. A glaze is brushed on in a strie manner, and then distressed with steel combs while still open, creating a narrow, stripelike finish. Several passes with the comb create a softer, more fabriclike appearance. Use the patented steel combs or make your own from rigid materials, such as gasket rubber from an auto supply store, to decorate a variety of surfaces. An example of this technique is shown right and on page 57.

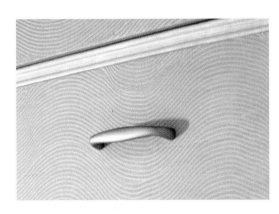

MATERIALS

water-base paints: latex eggshell (base coat), oil base satin enamel (for coloring glaze concoction)

mineral spirits

oilbase glazing liquid

TOOLS

basic layout and painting tools (see page xx)

China-bristle brushes

steel combs

paper towels

INSTRUCTIONS

1. Brush on the glaze in a strie manner, which is similar to wall dragging (see page 65).

2. Hold the comb to the surface at approximately a 30-degree angle and pass through the open glaze to distress it. After each pass, wipe the comb clean with a paper towel clean before proceeding.

3. Allow the glaze to dry at least overnight. Glaze and pass again in the cross direction to create a gingham effect.

BURLAP VARIATION

• For a burlaplike strie pattern, wrap the comb with a paper towel.

• When the glaze is dry, pass again in the cross direction with the towel-wrapped comb.

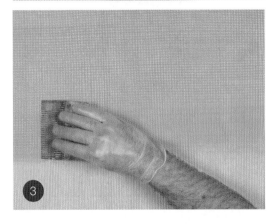

COLOR FORMULA (left to right):
khaki, linen white

THE STIPPLED LOOK

Stipple effects disperse glazes in a fine, blended pattern. A glaze concoction is applied with a brush, and then stippled with a separate brush, which is wiped frequently to avoid a buildup of material. A lightly loaded stipple brush can also be used to apply glaze in a style that results in a softer, clouded appearance. Large, high-quality brushes are necessary for a wall job where maximum blending is desired. This simple-looking effect—an evenly stippled wall—is the hardest faux finish to achieve. An example of this technique is shown below and on page 56 (top).

MATERIALS

water-base latex eggshell (base coat)

oil-base satin enamel (glaze concoction)

mineral spirits

oil-base glazing liquid

TOOLS

basic layout and painting tools (see page 26)

China bristle brushes

stipple brushes (various sizes; see page 25)

INSTRUCTIONS

1. Apply glaze in a dynamic pattern on trim work. Do not flood the recessed areas of the work, as the glaze will dry darker there (although this dark effect might be desired).

2. Hold the brush like a potato masher and stomp the surface to distress the glaze. (Old-time decorators call this technique *scumbling*.)

EVENLY UNEVEN

Remember that these are hand-applied finishes, and variation is part of the charm. "Evenly uneven" is the goal, but as a work session progresses, tired hands may cause changes in the patterning from a heavier application of glaze or a shift in the technique. Stand away from your work frequently to observe any unwanted changes, which can detract from the final finish. Beware of the painting environment; avoid hot, dry conditions, drafts, and direct sunlight to prolong the open time of paint and glaze mixtures.

FRENCH BRUSH

Use the French brush technique for wall glazing in soft pastel colors or more striking deep-tone combinations, always keeping the contrast between glaze and ground subtle.

MATERIALS

water-base matte paint: light cream (base coat), midtone sage green (glaze concoction)

water-base glaze (with a long open time)

TOOLS

basic layout and painting tools (see page 26)

high-quality Chinex brushes, 3" (7.5 cm) or 4" (10 cm) wide

INSTRUCTIONS

1. Load the brush with a moderate amount of glaze.

2. Cover the painting surface until the glaze is depleted by starting at the top of a wall and working towards the bottom. Glaze is applied lightly in a criss-cross pattern. Avoid overloading the brush, which leads to drips and runs. Frequently stand back to check that the glaze application is not drifting. Take care not to overlap the glaze application, as those areas will dry dark.

COLOR FORMULA: cream (top), green glaze (bottom)

A variety of brushes and combs awaits the faux artiste.

real faux

Faux in French means fake, or imitation. *Faux bois* and *faux marbe,* at their best, dare us to touch to make sure they are real—which, of course, they aren't. To achieve these treatments, single-step glazing techniques recombined, deceiving the eye with painted wood and painted marble effects.

A spectacular wood-grained mural brings intimacy to the harsh white surrounds of this modern environment. A large pattern was transferred to the wall four times, creating the repetition of the treescape, which was inspired by the prairie style of the early twentieth century. Each area of the pattern transfer was then patiently masked and grained with fast-drying glazes.

Right: The best faux finishers can create convincing painted versions of the multitude of real marble from around the world. A close-up of this faux *Breccia* accurately replicates the traffic jam of pulverized rock fragments that characterize this type of marble.

Facing page: Black-and-white *faux-marbe* columns on a grand scale were expertly painted, and then finished with multiple clear coats, rubbed smooth with fine sandpapers, and polished with wax. Not only the appearance, but the actual feel of marble, completes this deception.

This tabletop features a grouping of painted marble, inlaid adjacent to bronze banding. Belgian Black is a classic marble technique for furniture; careful attention is paid to the natural flow of veins over the table's molded, contoured edge.

This detail from a home technology center was constructed of high-density particleboard and economical pine moldings. Steel combs were used for the straight grains, and paper towels for the inlaid burl grain in the panel's faux walnut look. Note how the surface was carefully laid out and sectioned off to suggest the smaller pieces of wood normally used for rail and panel construction.

Wood-graining tools and color combinations inspired this painted wall finish. The final look is one of narrow slats of wood, which suggest a modern Scandinavian décor. Wood colors and soft textures always warm any area of the home.

Above: Various grains of blond mahogany appear in the painted surface of this home library. The crotch grain in the door panels imitates the expensive cuts of mahogany veneers, which are obtained by carefully slicing the branches of a tree. Lemon-gold metallic paint details the panel moldings.

Left: This post-and-beam construction is a visual artifice. Areas of the walls were taped, base coated, and grained in an oak pattern. The beams complement the contours of the room. A bit of sky peeks from behind a frame of the carefully laid-out, octagonal window. Half of the window frame sections are taped and grain treated. After they have been allowed to dry, the other half of the window frames is then taped, and the painting completed.

The *faux bois* beams and mantel further enrich the strong, red wall paint. First, tigerlike stripes are glazed across the direction of the grain. Next, a lightly distressed strie is applied in the direction of the grain, followed by several coats of clear finish.

These standard, flat garage doors were expertly grained in sections so they now appear to be constructed of joined board, surrounded by rail and stile. Painted highlights and shadows, including the grooves between the boards, add realistic touches. Painted-on iron strap hinges, door pulls, and round-headed nails complete the effect.

Poplar and pine millwork, typical of new construction, is grained in multiple steps and clear-finished to suggest the rare and far more expensive European walnut. The panels on the window wall received a burl graining of the same species.

■ **PROFILE**

Jean-Luc Sable, FRANCE

Faux finishers call it French style: an emphasis on the precise reproduction of materials. Mastery of this style demands extremely close study of woods and marble…and years of practice. Many layers of finishing, which often mix oil- and water-base mediums in different steps, result in the highest level of decorative painting. *Faux* does not mean a cheap imitation, but rather a highly-skilled deception.

French artisans enjoy a reputation, both historic and contemporary, as the best among faux finishers. In centuries past, these artisans traveled from Paris, spreading their craftsmanship across the European continent and to the New World. French decorating in the palaces of Sweden and Russia are now part of those countries' historical treasures.

Students of the French style seek a master-level education at the few select schools still in operation in Europe. This includes serious study for several years, with rigorous coursework in art theory and hands-on practice. Over their course of study, students produce a number of professional-level canvases.

The French style is excellent for matching existing finishes, such as wooden baseboards painted in imitation of marble mantels. Europe offers plenty for the faux enthusiast in many nineteenth-century-era restaurants, hotels, and other public buildings. Many architectural spaces are nearly living museums.

Jean-Luc Sable was voted France's Best Craftsman of the year in 2000, the highest award his country bestows, and an indication of how seriously France takes its decorative painting. He teaches extensively and applies his high-caliber skills in numerous commissions in many countries.

Facing page: An extravaganza of faux marbe is stunning in the ballroom of this residence. Strong-colored marble is surrounded by softer beige renditions, offering visual relief on a busy wall. Gilding with real gold leaf for detailing accompanies the rich surface treatments.

Left: This impressive trompe l'oeil trellis panel exhibits the painter's mastery of basic faux finishes. Strie techniques enhance the aged wood; the entire piece was painted on a softly stippled background.

Below: Curio cabinet paintings represent collections of personal items. This theme has enjoyed popularity since the time of the Dutch masters, and faux finishers today continue the tradition. Sable's version shows how surface imitation—in this case, wood and leather—are important tools for getting results.

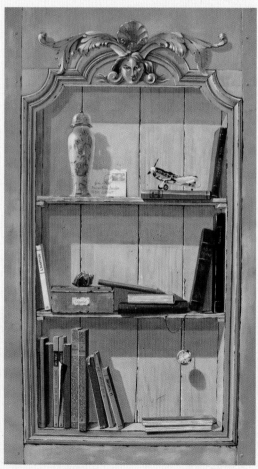

imitating nature:
marbleizing and wood-graining

Imitation marble achieved great sophistication in the decoration of the Baroque-era palaces of European nobles. Techniques that exactly imitate marble evolved to decorate ceilings where real marble was too heavy for practical use. Many a penny-pinching noble found utility in decorating on a more modest budget, and painted imitation spread widely. *Faux marbe* describes the exact imitation of real marble, whereas marbleizing is using the inspiration of marble to render attractive decoration with no exact material in mind.

Once the marbleizing technique is mastered, different methods can be combined using careful layout, producing impressive results.

veining technique

Marble veins come in many shapes and sizes. Faux finishers master veining through years of practice and observation of the real material. Their advice is to keep the veining medium thinned, so it flows readily from the tool. Hold the veiner loosely, as a conductor might hold a baton. (The veiner should not be held as though it's a pencil; this creates an overly tight, artificial-looking line.) Keep the veining networks angular and broken—not continuous lines, and not curvy. Work quickly. Think of veins as streams of liquid, which is what they were during formation, millions of years ago.

Painting veins is an important skill for marbleizing. Liner brushes and larger bird feathers are important tools for this process.

Avoid holding the tool like a pencil, which produces an artificial result.

Hold the brush loosely, with your palm curled and facing the work.

Pull the loaded tool toward you in a jagged, naturally contoured line.

COLOR FORMULA: linen white (above left), mixed gray (above right); mixing sequence for gray (below)

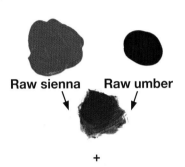

Raw sienna   **Raw umber**

+

White

↓

Midtone neutral

MARBLEIZING

To imitate Carrara marble, paint an off-white ground. Add a soft gray glaze, clouding it with paper towels, and then paint the veins with the same glaze. Carrara's coloration has a cold, blue cast. For a slightly warmer color palette, use a half-tone linen white as a base coat. For the gray midtone, mix a bit of raw umber into raw sienna, adding white to tint this dark tone to a midvalue. Dilute the grayish paint with approximately six parts glazing liquid. An example of this technique is shown on page 78.

MATERIALS

water-base eggshell paint: half-tone linen white (base coat, created by adding 50 percent white to linen); midtone gray (mixed with raw sienna and raw umber to gray, then tinted with white; for glaze concoction)

glazing liquid (with a long open time)

TOOLS

basic layout and painting tools (see page 26)

natural sea sponges

liner brushes (for veining, feathers can be substituted)

paper towels

BLENDING WET LAYERS

Working wet-into-wet produces better blending of layers when marbleizing small projects such as tabletops. This is less feasible on vertical surfaces such as walls, where a heavy load of material will start to sag.

INSTRUCTIONS

1. Color-wash the majority of the surface with the glazing concoction. Rub the wash heavily with a paper towel to disperse the glaze in a cloudlike manner, leaving pockets of base coat showing, or *daylighting*, on about 20 percent of the surface. The result should be very subtle. For larger projects, work in 3'-square (.9 sq m) square areas at a time.

2. While the glaze is wet, dab a few clouded areas with more of the same glaze, and blend again with a paper towel.

3. Wrap your index finger in the paper towel, and drag it through the still-wet glaze in a few areas to create negative veins.

4. Soften negative veins carefully with a paper towel or a blending brush.

5. Distress with paper towels, using a lighter touch, to produce slightly darker drifts. Remember that glazes become darker as they dry, so go lightly. More can be added later.

6. Pour a small amount of the mother glaze into a small cup, and add a few drops of water, which allows it to flow more easily from a brush. Feather or brush in some vein networks, avoiding the daylighted, base-coated areas.

7. While the veins are still wet, soften them with a crumpled paper towel or a softening brush. Do this over small areas at a time. Leave them to dry overnight, then finish the work with at least three coats of gloss acrylic varnish.

COLOR FORMULA: brown (top right), terra-cotta (bottom left), wood stain (bottom right)

WOOD-GRAINING

The imitation of wood dates at least from the time of King Tutankhamen, whose tomb featured painted wood furniture that imitated desirable grains.

After the Great Fire of London in 1666, a royal decree reserved oak exclusively for ship construction. An English grain-painting tradition evolved to satisfy the taste for oak. Other, more obtainable woods were painted to look like oak, with such great skill that most people believe the furnishings in present royal palaces to be not faux, but real oak. Some examples of this technique can be seen on pages 72–75.

MAHOGANY

Wood-graining at its best requires a variety of specialized tools and techniques. Getting the colors right is a major part of the task. The world of wood has a more limited palette than is typically used in home decoration. Mahogany wood comes in a variety of cuts (grains), which are popular in all kinds of cabinetry, furniture, and floor constructions.

A midtone terra-cotta, either pink- or orange-hued, serves as the base. A deep-toned brown paint mixed with 6 parts acrylic glaze is used in the banding step. A concoction of heavy-bodied wood stains diluted with 2 parts oil glaze finishes the overglazing. Mahogany stain is very red, and is best quieted by adding half a measure of Provincial wood stain for the final graining step.

MATERIALS

terra-cotta eggshell latex paint (base coat):
deep brown (for first glazing step)

oil-base stain (for second glazing step)

water-base glaze (with a short open time)

oil-base glazing liquid

mineral spirits

water-base varnish

TOOLS

basic layout and painting tools (see page 26)

Chinex-bristle brushes (for latex glaze)

China-bristle brushes (for oil-base glaze)

softening brush

paper towels

emery sandpaper

INSTRUCTIONS

1. Apply two coats of terra-cotta acrylic base coat and allow to dry.

2. Apply the banding glaze irregularly over the surface in the direction of the grain.

3. Roll a paper towel into an irregular-shaped band and hold it parallel to the tip of your fingers. Drag it gently over the glazed surface to disperse in a banded manner. Allow your fingertips to occasionally bear down hard, clearing the glaze from the base coat.

4. Feather the glaze by whisking with a softening brush in the direction of the grain. Allow to dry.

5. Drag the oil glaze made with wood stains over the surface in an even manner.

6. While the glaze is still open, distress it by flogging with a fine-haired, China-bristle brush. To flog, hold the brush with the ferrule parallel to the surface and gently tap the surface. After each tap, move the brush along in the flogging position for the next area. As in marbleizing, apply glaze on a small area at a time while the glazes are still open and workable.

7. After two days of drying, sand very lightly with a 400- to 600-grit, fine emery paper to remove grittiness. Wipe clean. Be careful not to cut through the glazes with too heavy a sanding touch. Finish with two coats of acrylic satin varnish.

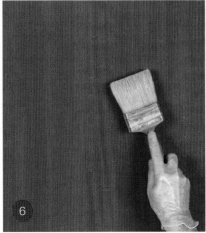

old materials, new twists

Venetian plasters are well suited for all color schemes. The texture plasters, or *muds*, are applied with a variety of techniques to add real relief to wall and ceiling surfaces. Marblelike qualities can be imparted with a trowel and polish, or textured surfaces can be finished with basic glazing techniques, enhancing the results with an old-world look.

The walls of this ancient grotto received several layers of texture, followed by several applications of glaze.

Plasters can be applied and finished many ways. Seasoned craftsmen often guard their methods, reluctant to share the fruits of experience. Here, the second plaster step, often called the *texture coat,* was troweled in a decidedly vertical manner. A neutral-tone ceiling in a flat beige paint softens the weight of such a dramatic finish.

Left: The deep blue sea shades are always a possibility for a powder room. Fish patterns were traced onto stencils for several layers. Plasters colored heavily with metallic powders were then applied in steps, and burnished along with the mother-of-pearl background.

Facing page: Very small amounts of gold mica powders were mixed into wax, which was then used for the final polishing step. The use of mica metallics in the plastering process adds a realistic reference of the metallic drifts found in real stone. A little goes a long way; too much metallic can be overwhelming.

Classical elements in this setting reference traditional decoration, with a somewhat contemporary feel. Venetian plasters were popular in Italy for hundreds of years, and the material is used in more modern homes as well.

Right: One must observe the process of decorative plastering to believe that movement in the finish is not a result of different-colored muds. The character of this wall was determined by the mud application and subsequent burnishing.

Facing page: Different textured surfaces were finished with a variety of glazing techniques for this futuristic bedroom. Custom color-staining techniques provide some unusual wood finishes, which tie those elements into this imaginative décor.

A knock down that was base-coated with silver metallic paint was then glazed lightly in several steps with transparent metallic glazes. The resulting wall has an extremely complex appearance, imitating a matrix of precious stone.

The texture coat of plaster in this niche was troweled on, and then distressed in a chip-chop manner. The pronounced marble look is enhanced by a final polishing and buffing with wax. The glasslike surface is nearly reflective.

The plaster batch was tinted slightly to yield this off-white wall decoration. Care must be taken with such light treatments to avoid dark marks left on the surface by careless application. With this in mind, plaster workers sand the edges of their trowels until they are round.

The soft textures of tile and wood nicely complement the perceived texture in the cornice area.

The knock-down method is the most common texture technique. Stucco-texture paint is troweled or rolled on with a thick-nap roller. Crumpled newspaper is pushed into the wet mud in a stipple motion, resulting in sharp peaks of relief. A tapered knife is then lightly pulled against the still-wet stucco, knocking it down to blunt the peaks.

Ronnie Soubra, LEBANON

Islamic art traditions stem from AD 622, when the founding of the religion and conquering of Muslim armies spread the traditions rapidly throughout the Mediterranean basin east to Asia proper. No other style traces its origin so close to a particular moment in time.

Islamic law prohibits the depiction of living creatures, and discourages artistic efforts for anything except the embellishment of practical objects. Traditional Islamic art is best studied in elaborately decorated manuscripts filled with calligraphy; or carvings on metal weaponry, dinnerware, and mosques. The restrictions on form and a mastery of mathematics shaped a distinctive style, which relies on geometric shapes for decoration. Natural forms such as tree branches and leaves influenced designs as Islamic art evolved, but were expressed in ever-more abstraction. Fantastic patterning, combined with strong colors, achieved refined levels of beauty. More recent Islamic art shows a definite return to realism, with modest concessions depicting plants and flowers.

Islam was embraced by many cultures, from the Ottoman Turks and Persian dynasties to the Moorish kingdom in Spain. Each group contributed traditional decorative arts to the style, resulting in notable regional expressions. The revival of arts in Europe during the Middle Ages borrowed from this ascendant culture, which we now recognize as Gothic style. Faux finishers borrow from these traditions.

The Alhambra of Spain is one outstanding example of Islamic artistic achievement. Wall tiles, columns, domes, and floors all feature exceptional polychrome detailing, with not one spot left behind. Geometric patterns repeat from the center, but never absolutely; they morph slightly as the pattern repeats, confounding mathematicians. The building is a stencil-pattern book for any faux finisher.

Ronnie Soubra works throughout the Middle East, from Dubai to Cairo, Egypt, and in her hometown, Beirut. She couples her university education in art with plenty of ambition to master the rapidly evolving products of the faux revival. She mixes pattern with many faux finishes for a trademark style that clearly expresses regional traditions.

Left: A limited palette is important for creating regional themes. The Mediterranean earth tones of umbers and sienna decorate a Tuscan as well as a Moorish theme.

Below: This historical Turkish treatment illustrates the skill of workmen from another time and the riot of nonfigurative Islamic patterns, which colors Soubra's approach.

Facing page: There is no chance of confusing this place with New York or Paris. It is Damascus, where the damask pattern and fabric style originated. This contemporary painted extravaganza departs from strict Islamic art tradition by featuring a bit of representational design, rather than just strict patterning.

textures and plasters

Venetian plasters create the illusion of texture by subtle reflections in the surface. Polish them and they assume an appearance of marble, with the surface quality of real stone. Texture paints are available in sand and smooth stucco, and can be distressed to create a number of interesting effects. Textures may be painted and glazed for cavelike results.

TEXTURE-PAINT
A TUSCAN KITCHEN

MATERIALS

water-base paints: latex primer tinted mustard, sand texture paint, smooth-texture paint, stucco-texture paint

mustard eggshell latex (for coloring glaze)

latex glazing liquid (with a long open time)

TOOLS

basic layout and painting tools (see page 26)

plaster knives (various sizes)

plaster trowel

large exterior siding brush

sponges, water, and towels (for cleaning tools)

sponge and tray (for color washing)

CHOOSE THE HIGH-END MUD

Lower-quality texture mediums cannot be glazed unless they are applied over a base coat, as the glaze medium will absorb and be blotchy. Higher-quality muds receive glazes directly without absorbing them.

COLOR FORMULA, left to right: mustard yellow, sand texture, smooth texture, yellow ochre

INSTRUCTIONS

1. Prime raw walls or base coat with any light-tone beige formula, then let dry completely.

2. Apply sand-texture paint with a large brush in a random manner to most areas. Let dry.

3. With a trowel, apply a layer of smooth, stucco-texture paint unevenly over three quarters of the surface, allowing some patches of the previous sand-painted areas to remain exposed. Work only 3' (.9 m) areas at a time before proceeding to the next step.

4. Within a few minutes of application, place a flat trowel on the wet mud and pull it away from the wall, making a peaked texture on the surface.

5. Smooth over the peaks with a taping knife to knock down the high points, leaving smaller pockets that allow the sand paint to daylight. Continue over the entire surface. Let this heavy application dry at least overnight, maybe longer depending on conditions.

6. For an aged look, apply a very transparent, earth-tone glaze, and rub vigorously to allow color remnants only in the pitted and recessed areas. Additional glazing steps can be applied and blended to make the surface more complex.

NOTE ON SURFACES

Texture paints and plaster are extremely messy to work with; surfaces must be thoroughly covered and protected.

VENETIAN PLASTER

Venetian plasters are best applied in a single color. Surfaces must be level and free of imperfections to receive these highly revealing finishes. The slightest nail pop or dent screams after the final polishing.

Color choices can be made from manufacturer's charts or approximated in paint stores, using colorants from the universal pigments.

Apply plasters with drywall-taping spatulas whose sharp corners have been sanded so they are rounded. This will avoid scratching the surface during application. Plastering spatulas are available at many suppliers.

COLOR FORMULA: mustard yellow paint (left), mustard yellow Venetian plaster (right)

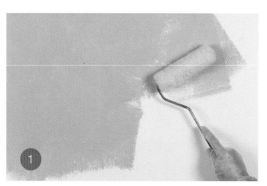

MATERIALS

mustard yellow Venetian plaster

water-base paint: latex flat mustard yellow (base coat, approximates Venetian plaster color)

TOOLS

basic layout and painting tools (see page xx)

knives (various sizes for applying plaster)

sponges (various)

water and paper towels (for cleaning tools)

emery paper (optional)

INSTRUCTIONS

1. Paint existing walls or prime new ones with any low- to flat-sheen latex paint that approximates the finished color. Allow to dry. A tinted base coat ensures that thin areas of plaster will not create a disagreeable contrast with the wall.

2. Load a modest amount of plaster on the trowel, and spread the scratch-coat thinly and evenly over the entire surface. Hold the spatula at approximately a 20-degree angle to the surface. The underlying wall color can daylight through this very thin application of plaster.

3. Wipe the tools often to remove material, and never replace small portions of unused plaster in the container. Dry bits of plaster scratch the surface, and will contaminate the mother batch.

4. Apply a texture coat of plaster over the entire surface by using a slightly thicker application of the same material, leaving slight voids and recesses. The areas that remain unfilled from this pass will be leveled with subsequent steps, creating the beauty of the finish. Minor differences in texturing create noticeable differences when the plaster is polished. Allow the texture coat to dry for a few hours, depending on conditions.

5. Apply two or three very thin finish coats over the texture coat. This is a somewhat exhausting process. Each coat will bring the surface gradually to life. Small voids and recesses in the texture will appear slightly different in color. If the surface is slightly bumpy from a careless application, it can be sanded to smooth with a 400- to 600-grit emery paper, in a circular motion.

6. After one scratch coat, one texture coat, and at least three finish coats, the smooth surface can be burnished to a greater sheen by rubbing it vigorously with the flat side of a clean spatula at a 30-degree angle to the surface. The more rubbing, the greater the final sheen. This will produce a marblelike appearance.

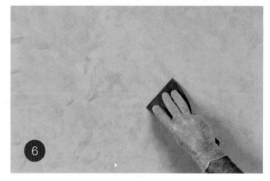

COMBAT THE CRUST

A damp rag over the plaster container keeps it from drying out and forming a crust. Having a large bucket of clean water and some old towels nearby allows for easy and frequent cleaning of the spatulas. Preventing a crust in the mud or on the spatulas during application ensures a smooth surface, which minimizes sanding.

stencilwork
with striping

Stencils speed the application of patterns on a wall. Any decorating style—not just trademark country—can be enhanced by the use of stencils. Stripes are good choices for stairwells, where their vertical geometry complements the space. Enormous stripes in very subtle contrast enhance a family room without getting formal. Sideways stripes also offer interesting possibilities that play with space.

Facing page: Applying stripes of different thicknesses requires careful measuring and double-checking of the layout. The flat-sheen stripes here were pebbled with a gloss varnish. (See the Technique Tutorial, Stripes with Stencils, page 110.)

Right: Carefully set, a large-format stencil was then struck with pewter metallic paint over an elaborately decorated ground.

A deep blue ground anchors a silver metallic stencil in this ode to Victoriana. Each large Mylar stencil was cut with two of the flower-vase patterns, one above the other. The silver paint was applied with a dry-brush technique. The corners of the room and the half pattern originating at the ceiling line were stenciled last.

Facing page: Stencils were used to apply this geometric pattern over a metallic faux colorwash of antique gold. Shadow detailing on the lower side of each layer of stenciling, done with a brush, helps the pattern *pop*.

The oldest stencils known, made of silk, were found in an ancient Chinese burial mound. This work makes a Far East statement when accessorized with black lacquer furniture. A three-bamboo-leaf stencil was set randomly and struck after the walls received evenly spaced shafts.

A gray midtone ground, stipple-glazed ever so softly, was stenciled with an off-white hue that was tinted with a small amount of the mother gray. An extremely large stencil, which patterned this project, requires careful handling, especially in a stairwell where the work is done from scaffolds.

Left: This armoire was base-coated in a dulled red, and then received a black enamel treatment, with a small amount of glaze added for slight transparency. When dry, the black was rubbed back with fine papers to expose the red ground for an antique look. The panels were base-coated with a variegated gold, and then stenciled with the same black. Expert preparation and varnishing makes this a fine family treasure.

Facing page: A large damask pattern stenciled in metallic gold adds to the richness of the real cherry wood. The pattern was struck against the wall using a stiff brush, lightly loaded. The arched and tight areas between the mirrors demand extra patience in registering and setting the stencils.

Transparent, silver metallic glazes were brushed, strie fashion, on areas taped with low-stick painter's tape. Each leaf frond was applied with the same glaze and brush technique, using individually cut stencils. Although limited in area, this was a time-consuming project.

These walls were treated to an off-white stencil pattern on a soft, color-washed gray ground. The bamboo trellis was also stenciled, then hand detailed for a more custom treatment. Hand-painted birds completed this multilayered finish.

A softly textured ground color, washed for a worn look, received transparent glazed patterning from the stencil strike. The overall look is of soft wear.

Metallic stencil paints detail a vivid red ground. The carpet on the ceiling provides impact in this otherwise austere décor.

Right: A midtone gray glaze, applied to masked areas in a broken strie technique, created wide stripes and broken color on the ceiling surfaces. A hand-painted floral pattern adorns the navy blue stripes, which are simply the base coat, left unglazed.

Facing page: These walls were base-coated in a deep blue, eggshell latex. A pewter metallic glaze was applied in masked-off areas and distressed with pieces of crumpled plastic sheets, which gave it a more cracked, fragmented texture than when distressing with paper towels. The stripes are different sizes, which demanded extra care in measuring the pattern on the wall.

A strie technique provided the vertical, stripelike, geometric pattern in this room. The glaze was applied irregularly, and dragged in a strie mode for a faux-denim look. A transparent, deep blue glaze followed a light blue, eggshell base coat, which was a light tint of the mother blue.

A close-up of Olssens's clouded ceilings highlights a blue to blue-gray color grouping. These colors are typical in the color schemes of Sweden's beautifully painted historic buildings.

■ **PROFILE**

Lotta Olssen, SWEDEN

As an architectural movement, Baroque featured heavily molded exterior surfaces that emphasized light and deep shadows. Baroque interiors were built simply, in anticipation of the elaborate painted treatments that would be applied. Expansive ceiling murals often featured celestial traffic jams of heroic characters, partially obscured by cloudbanks.

Trompe l'oeil moldings framed many of the murals, and artisans who specialized in that detail are receiving modern recognition for their skills. Superb marbleizing and wood-graining flourished, not as an economical alternative to the real thing, but as a celebration of the painter's skills.

The rise of Sweden as a world power during the Gustav period featured frantic construction in the north, creating a taste for continental culture. Sophisticated decorating from France arrived with hired workers, whose expertise adapted to a more

Swedish palette of colors, and a bit less fussy, more loosely executed technique. A distinctive Swedish style of painted decoration evolved.

Draw a straight line to Lotta Olssen, who shoulders a ladder onto the best of modern Sweden's treatments. Olssen is not only a master mentor to aspiring faux finishers at the celebrated Palm Fine Arts studio in Norrköping, but paints major commissions when she has time. Her work blends the roots of her homeland's historic sensibilities with sorties into new arenas that showcase her faux painting skills.

And what about the Baroque? The term remains popular, describing rooms with heavy window treatments, elaborately carved furniture, sculptured moldings, and painted ornament. Stenciled damask patterns, shadowed leafy flourishes, and gilding are the contemporary painter's contribution to a modern Baroque style.

Foyers in Swedish apartment buildings often receive a deluxe treatment. Lotta's faux marbe treatment in these panels includes trompe l'oeil moldings, with corner stenciling and expert striping. Clouded ceiling openings—detailed with glaze color-washing and gold leafing on the molding relief—adds to the décor a beautiful blue, a color dear in many Swedish hearts.

Olssen's many skills include imaginative mural work. This very modern work in a similar setting still references traditional color sensibilities.

stripes with stencils

Stripes are a good fit in many design schemes; historically, their popularity is evident from images of interiors in fine artwork. The earliest known wallpaper includes stripe patterns. Designers in the Regency period in England decorated with soft, tone-on-tone, wide stripes. Empire style in Napoleon's France manifested itself in narrower, high-contrast striping with striking effect. Victorians took it forward and embellished it, adding all sorts of elaborate patterning to stripe grounds.

Both of the following tutorials demonstrate stripes combined with stencils. Stripes are laid out and finished before moving on to the stencil steps. The stripes can be left as wall finishes in their own right. In the home, leaving stripes in some areas and finishing with stencils in adjacent areas creates what is called *companion finishes* in the trade.

The first technique finishes with a border stencil, which aligns with the edges of the stripes, making it easier to place smaller stencils. The second construction employs a large damasklike stencil, which sets into the middle of a wide stripe. The larger stencils are more difficult to handle and place, involving layout points to register the exact placement of the stencil.

the egyptian stick method

Sophisticated engineering skills, including precise measurements, were employed to build the great pyramids at Gaza. Huge, stone blocks were fit together so tightly that a piece of paper cannot be placed between them. The Egyptians used sticks of various sizes and calibrations to transfer and check their measurements.

This method can be adapted for planning stripe placement. First, use a ruler to determine the increments on a scrap of oak tag. Use this "stick" with its marks for transferring the stripes to the walls with light pencil marks. Sticks work particularly well when the stripe increments are not in even, round measurements. Premeasured shapes, such as squares for checkerboard floors, also speed layout projects.

Create an Egyptian stick for easier placement of stripes on walls.

FRENCH BRUSH STRIPE WITH BORDER CHAIN

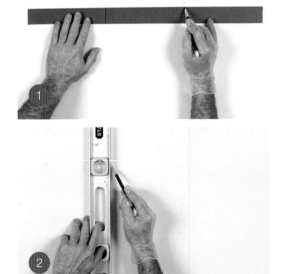

COLOR FORMULA: light cream (top), sage green (lower left), gold metallic (lower right)

MATERIALS

water-base matte paint: light cream (base coat), midtone sage green (glaze color)

mica paint: metallic gold

glazing liquid (with a short open time)

TOOLS

basic layout and painting tools (see page 26)

Mylar and transfer patterns (for stencils)

orange core tape, 1½" (3.8 cm) wide

synthetic sponges

carpenters' levels (various sizes)

Egyptian stick (see tip box, page 111)

INSTRUCTIONS

1. Measure points on the wall at 8" (20.3 cm) intervals, keeping the marks light. Place stripe points above the eye line because they tend to be visible when the work is done. Start and then stop the layout in the least important corner of the room—for example, behind a door.

2. With a level, lightly pencil guidelines vertically on the wall to determine the stripe borders. Place a scrap of tape in each stripe that is to be glazed. It's easy to get confused and glaze the protected area instead of the intended stripe area.

3. Place wide tape slightly outside of penciled lines. Erase lines with a soft gum eraser. This also burnishes the tape against the surface, which prevents bleeding. The stripe will be made with a transparent glaze, which allows any lingering pencil lines to show. Make sure to erase the pencil lines completely before glazing.

REUSE THE TAPE

To get the most out of expensive blue tape, allow the medium to dry before carefully removing it. This prevents the tape from curling, and it can usually be reused several times.

on the level

Lightweight, aluminum I-beam carpenter's levels are the painter's choice to hold aloft for hours at a time. Masons' heavy wood levels tire the arm—and test the pocketbook with their much greater cost.

When the level bubble is between the black hash marks, the vertical or horizontal is *true.* Being *level* means true for horizontal. Being *plumb* is true for vertical. Wrap the ends of the levels with tape to prevent black marking on the walls, which is difficult to remove. Cut small moldings and gently force them into the I-beam to allow the level to stand off the wall. The level can then be used as a straight-edge guide for a liner brush without smearing the paint.

Stippled metallic paints over a tinted ground create this contemporary style striped finish.

4. Mix the soft green paint to 3 parts fast-drying glazing liquid, and French brush the stripe areas. Remove the tape carefully at any time. The finish can be considered complete as a simple stripe.

5. When the entire room is striped and all tape is removed, place a chain stencil slightly below the ceiling line, centering it on the border between the stripes.

6. Strike the stencil with a gold metallic paint, mixed into approximately 5 parts gloss acrylic varnish, based on samples. This stencil medium dries quickly, allowing the next stencil down to be placed in about thirty minutes. Working with at least eight stencils allows many stripes to be done at once, and allowed to dry.

SPEEDY TEAMWORK

One person setting the stencils and one person striking the stencils speeds the project tremendously.

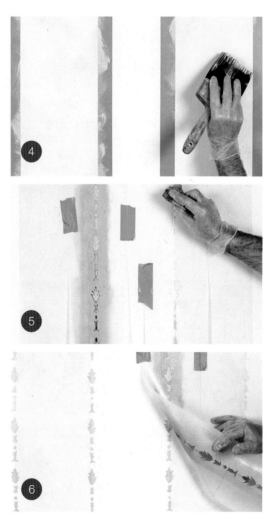

COLOR FORMULA (clockwise from top, left): light blue (base coat), dark blue (wide stripe), cream (narrow stripe), platinum mica (stencil)

STRIPES WITH PEWTER STENCILING, DAMASK STYLE

MATERIALS

water-base matte paint: light blue (base coat), darker blue (stripe), cream (stripe)

mica paint: platinum (stenciling)

TOOLS

basic layout and painting tools (see page 26)

carpenters' levels (various)

Egyptian stick (see tip box page 111)

orange core tape, 1" (2.5 cm) and 1½" (3.8 cm) wide

mini-roller, 4" (10 cm) wide

natural sea sponge

synthetic sponge

paint tray

stencil, damask pattern, or style of choice on Mylar

INSTRUCTIONS

1. Apply a base coat to prepared and primed walls and let them dry. Using primer is a necessary step to ensure that tape removal does not damage the surface.

2. Lightly mark the stripes around a room with premarked sticks of 7" (17.8 cm) and 9½" (24.1 cm) lengths. The arrows on the stick should always point toward the ceiling.

3. Pencil in stripes very lightly, using longer levels for full walls and smaller levels for tight spaces and around doors and windows.

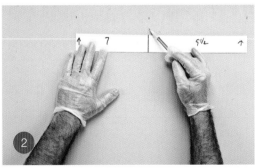

4. Place wide tape slightly outside of the penciled line, and smooth the edge with a finger to prevent paint from bleeding under it. Scraps of tape are important reminders of which stripes not to paint. Pencil lines need not be erased, because the painted (not glazed) stripe will cover them.

5. Paint the dark blue stripe with a mini-roller, then carefully remove the tape at any time.

6. In the wider stripe area, painted light blue, mark two 3" (7.6 cm) stripes, tape, and paint a light cream color twice with a mini-roller. Let dry.

7. Cut a natural sea sponge in half to apply a water-base, high-gloss varnish (not mixed with any color) in a pebblelike fashion over the entire wall. This dries almost immediately, providing a sparkle effect.

8. With a permanent marker, draw reference points on the stencil to aid in centering the stencil on the striped pattern. Start at the ceiling line, and center the stencil in the dark blue stripe. The pattern of the stencil should start ½" (1.3 cm) below the ceiling line. The top of the stencil is folded to fit snugly. Secure the stencil with several pieces of low-tack tape.

9. Mix 1 part platinum metallic paint to 4 parts high gloss varnish. Sponge on with a piece of synthetic sponge, taking care not to flood the surface and cause excessive bleeding under the stencil edges.

10. Check the stencil to assess your work. When finished striking the entire pattern, remove immediately to prevent gluing the stencil to the wall. Place the stencil two stripes away and continue. The next stripe cannot be stenciled immediately, because the stencil will overlap the wet paint, and smear.

over and under

Floors and ceilings are just neglected walls; faux finish them to create high-impact spaces. Softly fauxed backgrounds are an excellent stage for geometric, inlaid stone patterns, which are laid out, taped off, and faux-finished again with a selection of finishes. Bordering can serve on any surface of a room, and also for furniture decoration.

The classic checkerboard pattern is laid out with some simple math and a familiarity with layout tools such as templates. Simply glaze or marbleize the checkerboard pattern to impress your guests.

Despite the large grooves in this oak-plank floor, a checkerboard-painted marble disguises the ground and begs for closer inspection. See the Technique Tutorial, Checkerboard and Marble Floors, page 133.

Borders of real gold leaf and Chinese red decorate this vestibule on an unpolished Venetian plaster ground. Stenciling and hand painting provided the space with impact.

A gold metallic was the base coat for the entire ceiling, including the center medallion. Transparent glazing on the flat ceiling areas distressed the surface with a hammered look. The medallion remained solid gold for accent.

Simple-process glazing techniques were combined with some stenciling know-how to decorate a recessed ceiling niche. The niche background was an off-white paper towel, distressed with a midtone beige glazing concoction. Venetian plaster in a selection of closely colored muds created the vertical wall patterning. Color-washed, carved moldings soften the overall contrast of elements.

A small dome was leatherized with a dark base-and-glaze combination. A multistep stencil process was used to paint a faux medallion in a deep bronze metallic. The walls of the room, stippled earthy pink, display hand-painted ornament over the windows.

Wood graining and elaborate stencils appoint this atrium. The center medallion was color-washed, and the high-relief areas rubbed vigorously. The perimeter molding of brackets and crown was treated the same. The gray walls' light-tone glazing gives a look of texture that fits comfortably into the scheme.

Left: A deep red Venetian plaster was used as the base coat for a complicated stencil pattern, which was struck with gold mica powders, mixed in wax. The variation was intended for an old-world, faded look.

Below: Gold-finished trim work and panel elements border traditional *chinoiserie*, which is painting in a Chinese style. The scenes were painted with different transparencies of the same mother color. Clouding on the ceiling was also done with multistep glazing.

This ode to Victoriana indulges the pleasures of those days, which included decorating with an excessive use of pattern. True to period sensibilities, border patterns in line and stencil repeat inside of other borders in line and stencil.

Metallic paints added a realistic touch to the rusted ironwork, painted after clouds were added to this ceiling recess . Subtle textures and glazing on surrounding areas frame the artwork.

A sophisticated knowledge of glazes and perspective yielded this convincing trompe l'oeil ceiling, which looks like the inside of a dome, but is really on a flat surface. The stone balusters and their shifting shadows are especially convincing.

Facing page: A boy's bedroom displays a nautical theme with painted depth charts and a compass star. Splayed ceilings in second-level, dormered bedrooms offer particular challenges because they are neither walls nor ceiling. This clever treatment is simple in execution and attractive in the blue-and-green color palette.

Above: Members of the immediate household found their place in this subtropical rendition of the painted dome. This person has been captured for all time at a younger age.

Right: Renaissance Italians discovered subterranean caves called grottos hidden in their landscape. Their explorations revealed fantastically detailed wall painting from the time of the Romans. They imitated the ancient work, giving rise to a style called *Grottesca*. The style here is rendered enthusiastically.

Above: Pine floorboards were lightly sanded to dull the finish and ensure adhesion. A number of different stencils were overlaid in succession, each struck with a different color. Three coats of a high-quality, clear floor finish followed.

Facing page: The existing floor finish was dulled with a fine sanding. Transparent oil glazes, mother-colored with an oil stain, were stenciled and strie-brushed in masked areas. When dry, clear floor finishing followed.

MAKE SURE IT STICKS

Floor decoration can use a stained wood background as the base coat. Take care to ensure glazes *stick* by first testing an inconspicuous corner. When the stain is dry, cover it with a piece of low-quality tape, and rip the tape off quickly. If glaze is on the tape, you have adhesion failure.

Painted on concrete, this amoeba-shaped floor painting is inspired by natural plant forms. Tree branching is influenced by underlying mathematical principles, resulting in patterns familiar to all. This design can be envisioned as the tangle of wood growing up to the forest canopy.

■ PROFILE

Lucretia Moroni, ITALY

Even during the darkest moments of the Middle Ages, Italy never lost its connection with antiquity. An environment of Roman ruins and discarded objects from the Caesars' time prompted an ever-increasing artistic scrutiny of the past, while the present evolved into the Renaissance.

Masters such as Raphael cultivated a keen curiosity of the classic, evident in the decoration of the pope's chambers at the Vatican. Raphael had himself lowered into subterranean grottos to record and then recreate the painted ornament he found there, hidden from view for centuries.

The best artists of the day crafted furniture, musical instruments, and buildings alike. All required ornamentation, which the same artisans did with gilding and paint. Renaissance men such as Leonardo and Michelangelo could do it all.

Venice was then a world power, sending a fleet of craftsmen and culture throughout the Mediterranean. Venetians dominated the textile trade, patronized all arts, and filtered the influence of Islam as Europe's gateway. Elaborate geometry in Islamic design was observed, absorbed, and then regurgitated by artisans who decorated in the most opulent age of *Veneto*. Passions for art ran so high that a fistfight or stabbing might conclude a barroom discussion of some painter's merit.

Above: Moroni's mastery of European textiles manifests itself in this carpet-like floor treatment. Certainly not timid in employing pattern, the construction also speaks of a strong color sense and her determination to use it.

Below: The positive pattern of the strip wood between tiles and the filigree-inlaid pattern are remnants of the original floor finish. Transparent glazes for the stencil medium allow the actual grain of the underlying floor to remain evident.

The refinement of the Italian Renaissance dazzled invading French armies, which carried the style home, occasionally in the form of the Italian masters themselves. Other European countries had established traditions, as well.

Lucretia Moroni's roots extended as far back as thirteenth-century Bergamo, Italy. Her family name references the mulberry tree, which feeds the silkworms that her family imported for silk manufacturing. Her work draws upon intimate knowledge of textile design, combined with a knack for faux finishing. *Fatto a mano* (made by hand) fully describes her personal style, which focuses on superb craftsmanship and intricate patterns.

painted borders, floors, and ceilings

SPARKLE ON INLAID GRANITE

Use the following sparkle wall treatment as a soft foil for busy marbled baths. First, layout and sponge-paint the inlaid faux granite (see pages 63–65 for sponging instructions). Each of the pebbled layers gets progressively darker, hiding the previous process.

Spend some time considering the number of borders and their placement in a room before plunging in. In these multifinish projects, keep most of the finishes soft and only one strong. Too many busy finishes creates visual disharmony.

The walls need a good primer-sealer before base coating to avoid damage from ripping the extensive tape in this layout. Gloss acrylic varnish, used undiluted and mixed with metallic paints, is the glaze medium for all the steps in this finish. Bronze and pewter metallic paints, from extreme to modest transparencies, color the border elements.

A flat base coat is needed to maximize the sparkle of the gloss varnish. The gloss varnish dries very quickly, allowing the multistep layouts to move along. The layout procedure demonstrated can border ceilings, walls, or floors. First, base coat the walls with a quality, flat dove white, then allow to dry.

MATERIALS

water-base paints: flat dove white latex (base coat); gloss latex varnish: pebble finish and glaze additive for mica paints; metallic mica paints; warm silver (wide and inlaid border have different transparencies); antique bronze (narrow border accent)

TOOLS

basic layout and painting tools (see page 26)

orange core tape, 1" (2.5 cm) and 1½" (3.8 cm) wide

natural sea sponges (various sizes)

carpenters' levels (various sizes)

Egyptian sticks for borders (see page 111)

templates, square and Greek key

serrated knife

COLOR FORMULA Clockwise from top left: warm silver, silver, antique bronze, Greek key template, dove white

VARNISH SAMPLES

Clear finish should always be included in the sampling process. Especially on subtle-contrast faux work, the finish can be an important step.

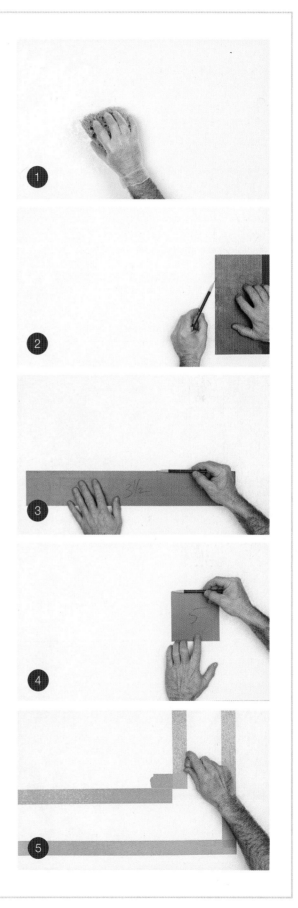

INSTRUCTIONS

1. With a serrated knife, cut a natural sea sponge in half to expose a flat surface. This will create an irregular pebble texture. Use the slightly dampened sponge to pebble the walls with gloss varnish. Be careful not to glop the barely visible, clear varnish on the walls; this will create drips, which are highly visible when dry. The finish imparts a pearly, sparkly quality that changes as the light and perspective varies.

2. On the first wall, measure 6" (15.2 cm) from the sides and, with a large carpenter's level, lay out a large rectangle (keeping the pencil lines light).

3. Cut a template from railroad board, 3½" (8.9 cm) wide and 16" (40.6 cm) long, to place inside the rectangle for the inner margin of the border.

4. Place a 5" (12.7 cm) -square template to establish the corner margins.

5. Stick 1½" (3.8 cm) blue tape on the outside and inside margins of the penciled border, keeping the pencil lines slightly exposed. Burnish the tape with a gum eraser to remove the guidelines. The border glazing steps are very transparent, so complete erasure is a must.

VARIATION

• For an inlaid border over an existing polyurethane finished floor, mask and lightly sand the bordered area. Use an oil-glaze concoction made with wood stains, which has very high adhesion to existing finishes. Decorate the border with a wood-graining technique. Polyurethane when dry for durability.

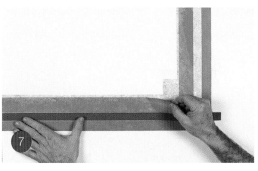

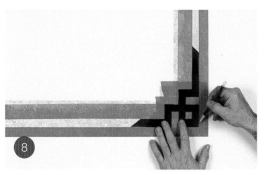

6. Mix warm silver metallic paint with gloss varnish to about a 1:3 ratio. Apply the pebble finish inside the taped border. Remove tape carefully when the paint is dry to reuse in step 7.

7. Place 1" (2.5 cm) -wide tape on the inside of the outside margin of the pebbled warm silver border. Use a ¼" (6mm) -wide stick to mark a channel on the inside of the repositioned tape. A 1" (2.5 cm) border channel is now masked inside the recently painted, wide border. The inside border is *not in* the center of the first border, but traced off-center to provide visual interest.

8. Trace and tape a fancy corner return with a Greek key template. Some careful tracing and cutting is needed here.

9. When all is taped and burnished, pebble with a 1:2 ratio of metallic silver to varnish. While still wet, pebble slightly with a 1:3 ratio of metallic bronze to varnish in an evenly uneven manner. This references the small dark flecks in granite. Carefully remove the tape when dry. An example of the completed Greek key technique is shown on page 130.

SPARKLE SUBSTITUTES

Substitute a soft marble background or color wash for the sparkle finish ground, and create border inlays in a different marble or glazing technique. This entire finish sequence also looks spectacular in various wood grains.

CHECKERBOARD
AND MARBLE FLOORS

Poor preparation penalizes the floor painter severely with adhesion failure. The best results are obtained on floors that are sanded to raw before painting. Avoid the temptation for excessive patching on floors. Patches will likely loosen when dry winter conditions cause the wood to shrink. Three base coats tend to fill a lot of the imperfections one is inclined to patch. If working over an existing floor finish, sand with rough paper such as 80-grit, clean, and then prime with a high-adhesion paint such as white shellac.

Use white shellac tinted linen white for the base coat. A popular brand is B-I-N, which provides super adhesion, dense opaque coverage, and quick drying. Three coats, acting as primer and base, are easily applied in one day. B-I-N dries with a sheen, making it an excellent base for glazing work. Use a respirator and a floor fan to ensure relief from the hazardous fumes. Plan to work toward an open door for easy exit. Allow to dry.

AUTHOR'S NOTE; *The first five steps are illustrated on an imaginary floor at reduced scale. In the real world, two people make the accurate measurement and laying out of any sizable room easy. A long straightedge is a valuable aid, but beware of using wood strips as they are usually slightly bowed, which can wreak havoc on accuracy. The last five steps illustrate the actual painting procedure.*

MATERIALS

white shellac, tinted linen white (base coat)

water-base: dark charcoal latex eggshell (dark squares); red, green, and white latex eggshell (gray marbleizing, for adding to glaze concoction)

latex glaze (with a short open time)

satin floor varnish

TOOLS

basic layout and painting tools (see page 26)

long straightedge

large templates, cut to size of desired squares and one isosceles triangle

orange core tape, 1½" (3.8 cm) wide

Egyptian stick (see page 111)

large carpenter's square

mini-roller

PADDED SADDLE

Floor painting can be a painful proposition, as it stretches the body in places seldom tried. Avoid exclusively kneeling, back bent over all day; shift frequently, rise and stretch, and lay or sit hip-wise on a piece of foam to maintain comfort.

COLOR FORMULA): linen white (top left), deep charcoal (top right), neutral (red mixed with green, then tinted with white)

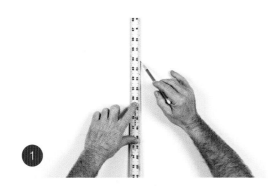

INSTRUCTIONS

1. Find the center point of the room. Assuming the room is a perfect rectangle (although this is not usually the case in older dwellings), measure halfway across from one wall at both ends of the wall, and place points with a pencil. Stretch a string connecting those points and trace a line with a long straight edge.

2. Repeat the process from the right-angle wall, tracing a line that bisects the room at a right angle to the original line. Use a large carpenter's square to check the right-angle intersection of the two lines.

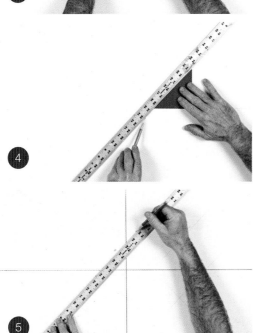

3. Cut a square from railroad board to the size of the desired checkerboards (13"–15" [33–38.1 cm] squares are best); lay it turned 45 degrees at the center of the room, aligning it as a diamond on the original layout lines, and trace lightly.

4. Extend and pencil-trace the square in all directions with the use of a long straightedge and a 45-degree wedge.

5. Complete the layout on the entire floor, using the square template and straightedge. Frequently place the square template in traced squares to ensure their accuracy. A drift of less than ¾" (1.9 cm) on any square is acceptable. The layout is never perfect, so don't make yourself crazy. If the squares start to become rectangles, erase the layout lines with warm water on a facecloth and start over.

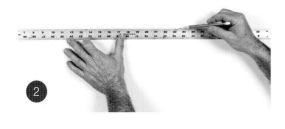

FAMOUS FLOORS

Van Cortland Manor, a historic Hudson Valley house in New York State, is the inspiration for the following painted floor. Evidence of it was found during restoration efforts, and talented finishers recreated it based on those findings. A similar painted marble floor can be seen in the great room at Gracie Mansion (the mayor's residence) in New York City.

6. When the layout is complete, tape over every other square, leaving the pencil lines slightly exposed. They will be painted out. Cut the corners carefully with a snap knife, changing blades frequently. Burnish the tape with an old credit card or single-edge razor to prevent paint from bleeding when the checkerboards are base coated.

7. Add a touch of linen white to black, making a deep, slightly warm charcoal gray, and paint squares with a mini-roller. When the paint is dry, pull up and dispose of the tape to reveal a checkerboard pattern.

8. Starting in one corner of the room, marbleize in the manner shown in Chapter 2 (on pages 78–81)

9. Overlooking the checkerboard pattern, marbleize the entire floor. If the mother glaze was mixed correctly, it will look dark against the light squares, and light on the charcoal squares, producing what looks to be two distinctly colored marbles. This is a classic example of color being influenced by its environment.

10. Add veining to either the light or dark squares to exaggerate the difference of the checkerboards. When dry, finish with at least 3 coats of acrylic floor varnish; oil polyurethane will amber, which is undesirable unless an antique look is desired.

GORGEOUS GRAY

Mix two complementary colors (such as green and red) until they create a neutral, and then add white to arrive at a midtone gray. Mix the midtone gray with three parts acrylic glaze. Grays created from complements surpass mixing black and white for beauty.

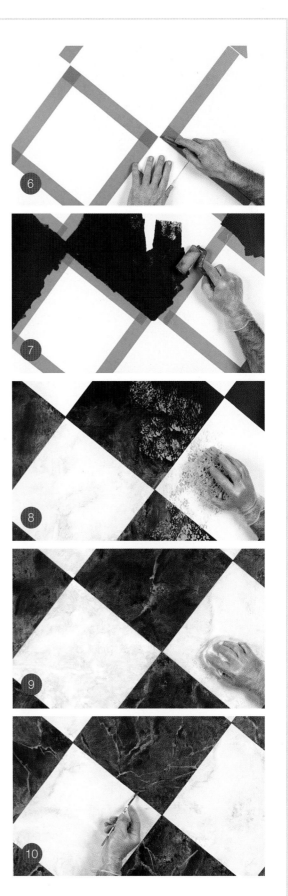

new looks old

Age speaks of wisdom and permanence. Thus, faux finishers eagerly hone skills that bestow value through the imitation of wear. The best efforts leave a viewer perplexed by the real nature of the subject. Use strie or dragged finishes on trim work and cabinetry to soften solid colors into elegant, antique looks. The deception increases with the layering of techniques.

Faux stone finishes also impart that *have-to-look-twice* ambience. Cut, dressed, limestone blocks in large sizes provide interesting wall finishes that put one in mind of a French chateau.

Left: It's best to paint faux stone in a large-size format. A little detailing, cracks, and chips add wear, but be cautious about overdoing it. Less is more!

Venetian plaster wall finishing was stenciled in an irregular pattern. Plaster provided the stencil medium, and was slightly sanded back when dry, resulting in a distressed look. Glaze color-washing on details such as brackets says "old."

Right: Heavy-pitted texture was color-washed with glazes to complement the other limestone elements in this kitchen hood and backsplash arrangement. Real limestone accumulates dirt in the pitting, which is impossible to remove. The glazing-over-texture technique mimics that condition accurately.

Facing page: A combination of colored Venetian plasters, applied in a broken, irregular manner, makes this corner look timeworn. Antiqued accessories and furnishings complete the mood.

Plaster formulas with metallic mica powders were mixed and highly burnished for a rough-sawn lumber vanity, with an unpolished edge on its countertop. The elements combine in an elegant, but aged-looking combination.

All surfaces are expertly aged in this study. Wood-graining and stencil techniques advance the years by rubbing with sandpaper and glazing over with a *good dirt* formula.

Above: Simple-process glazing work provided the decoration for the trim, walls, and ceiling medallion in this comfortable, timeworn dining room. A warm gray—not white—ceiling color quiets the scheme, and is an unspoken hero for this décor. Gold metallic paint effectively details trim elements.

Left: Patented products offer an array of options for the decorative painter. In many cases, the products substitute for the jealously guarded secrets of past finishers. Nowhere is this more evident than in the antiquing game. This new mirror was treated on the back with such a product, to appear aged and tarnished.

Above: These stenciled walls were rubbed, and the trim work strie-glazed and rubbed to allow the glaze to pool in the recesses. The wall below the chair rail and the ceiling were glazed and distressed to soften their contrast with the other elements. This total-surface finishing approach is the distressed look.

Right: These walls received a slightly embossed stencil pattern, with the application of texture paint, tinted brick red, as the stencil medium. An overall beige-glazed finish followed, and was rubbed while still wet, exposing the red highlights on the embossing.

Opposite page: New, painted off-white cabinetry was brush-glazed with a thick, brown concoction, and rubbed extremely hard to leave very soft, broken color overall, with dark puddling in the recesses. Old-world plaster glazing in this large space completes a deceit of time in this brand-new house.

■ PROFILE

Yaeko Kurimata, JAPAN

Japanese style for the home remains traditional—simple partitions with naturally finished post-and-beam wood construction. Great manifestations of their decorative skills come to us from the past as fabric designs and lacquer ware.

Lacquer was originally made from insects found exclusively on small trees of the sumac family. Crushed and processed elaborately, the *lac* finish was applied in dozens of successive coats, painstakingly polished along the way. Fine examples of the work survive from more than two thousand years ago.

Gold leaf was used for decoration on many of the objects. Leaf was pulverized and blown onto objects as dust. Carved relief was gilded or polychromed in minute detail for such finishes as *mokume* and *kogo*. Corpulent characters, knarled pines, and ocean waves appeared over time, planting themselves deep in decorative arts style.

Yaeko Kurimata wants her neighbors to reconnect with their roots and hire her to paint that past with her new faux methods.

Kurimata's education in textiles and graphic arts led her to further studies abroad, where a hobby of painting came to dominate her creative efforts. She returned to Japan, eventually starting a decorating company, faux painting restaurants and department stores.

Kurimata's Japanese commercial spaces tend to be European-inspired, such as a pastoral scene of Italy with hand-painted stone, or floral borders railroading around a textured wall that is color-washed in an old-world sensibility.

Sometimes Kurimata's decorative choices have roots closer to home. She references motifs from Japan's rich graphic traditions with a modern interpretation. Faux-finish techniques create a tranquil koi pond of goldfish luxuriating near lily pads; or a Japanese tea garden of solitude for a busy Tokyo night spot. *Urushi nuri,* traditional red and black lacquer work, flows as easily from her brush as marbleizing. She incorporates traditional symbols, such as turtles (which represent long life) and ocean waves (the fluctuations of fortune).

Clockwise from facing page: The Japanese home remains conservatively appointed with slightly textured walls and naturally finished wood. These doors are muraled with the traditional, much-loved motif of stormy waves, but with contemporary painting techniques.

Kurimata used strie-weave techniques with glazes for this faux-denim background. She gradually burnished the finish for a worn look. Trompe l'oeil stitching completes the denim deception with painted holes, highlights, and shadows. Traditional stenciled Japanese motifs allow the denim to peek through.

Goldfish are one of Kurimata's signature finishes, evoking centuries of Japanese tradition.

The Japanese cherish their traditional culture at home but embrace international style in their public spaces. A pastoral villa, complete with a row of poplars, was bordered with painted Roman ornament in monochrome. The combination of elements places us north of Tuscany, rather than in downtown Tokyo.

antiquing trim and walls

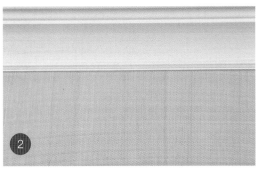

STRIE ON TRIM

Muddy, neutral glazes on off-white grounds decorate trim against dramatic wall effects. High contrast with a different color family provides a more country look.

The trim work in many homes is enameled with an acceptable off-white satin or semigloss paint. With these conditions strie can proceed, sparing the time and expense of base coating. The job is ready to go.

Mix a glaze concoction of 1 part mineral spirits to 2 parts commercial oil glaze and add the mother color as premixed, satin, oil-base paint. Alter the oil-base color by intermixing it with similar oil-base paints. Very transparent glazes generally serve the need of a strie finish. Do not hesitate to experiment with glaze paint mixtures of 3:1, ranging up to 50:1.

SAMPLE FOR TRANSPARENCY

MATERIALS

latex eggshell (base coat)
oil-base satin enamel (for coloring glazes)
mineral spirits
oil-base glazing liquid

TOOLS

basic layout and painting tools (see page 26)
China-bristle brushes (various sizes)
artist brushes
paper towels

INSTRUCTIONS

1. Mix, then drag a 4-part glaze to 1-part paint concoction. Allow it to dry overnight and then varnish.

2. Mix, then drag a 10-part glaze to 1-part glaze concoction. Allow it to dry overnight and then varnish.

3. Mix, then drag a 20-part glaze to 1-part glaze concoction. Allow it to dry overnight and then varnish.

4. Mix, then drag a 40-part glaze to 1-part glaze concoction. Allow it to dry overnight and then varnish

SAMPLE FOR DARK DETAIL

On a dragged, 20-part glazed molding (dried overnight), apply the same glaze with artist brushes on selected areas of the trim work. Alternatively, darken the mother glaze with a small addition of paint to create a darker accent.

SAMPLE FOR LIGHT DETAIL

Drag a 20-part concoction; while wet, wipe a part of the molding with a carefully folded paper towel to remove some of the still-wet glaze. The towel can be dampened with mineral spirits to increase the removal.

SAMPLE FOR AN ANTIQUE LOOK

Drag a 10-part concoction; while wet, wipe it vigorously from the entire surface allowing it to remain puddled in the recesses of the molding profiles.

SAMPLE FOR ELECTRIC COUNTRY

Mix and drag a 4-part concoction; while wet, drag a second old, worn-out brush through the glaze creating an uneven dispersion. This produces an almost wood-grained look.

GO WITH THE GRAIN

Always drag trim in the direction of the underlying wood grain. On cabinet stiles, place pieces of tape and burnish to make a crisp edge at the beginning and end of each stile, strie, and let dry. Protect the finished work with tape when continuing on the adjoining piece. When working trim, crowns, and base moldings in a corner, first strie a short length out of the corner before completing the longer run into the corner. This avoids bunching glaze in the corner, which is very difficult to clean up.

COLOR FORMULA:
midtone taupe (top left),
linen white (bottom left)

CUT AND DRESSED STONE

For this faux stone, apply a soft, color-washed background and then using liner brushes, grout in shadows and highlights. The most important aspect is the color mixing. Take care not to make the grout shadow too dark, as it will come forward to the viewer and appear as a wire fence against a gray daylight sky. Don't hesitate to make a series of samples to get the glazed background and grout contrast in balance.

Measure stone blocks 14" (35.6 cm) high and 18" (45.7 cm) long. Adjust the height within in this range for the actual size. (The blocks shown in this tutorial are not drawn to size in order to better illustrate multiple rows.)

Gray-to-beige tones work best as mother colors for the glaze. Again, test transparencies for the grout carefully, as the balance between the grout and wall glazing is paramount to the success of this deception.

Stone blocks stand alone as a wall finish, or make an excellent background for mural constructions.

MATERIALS

latex eggshell paints: linen white (base coat), midtone taupe (for coloring glaze concoctions)

two latex glazes (one with a long open time, one with a short open time)

TOOLS

basic layout and painting tools (see page 26)

carpenters' levels (various lengths)

two Egyptian sticks (one for stone length, one for stone width)

liner brush

sponges

INSTRUCTIONS

1. Apply two base coats of linen white, eggshell latex, and allow to dry.

2. Mix a midtone beige to 3 parts glazing liquid, and color-wash the walls as described in the single-process glazing tutorial (see pages 96–97). Allow to dry.

3. Measure the space between the floor and ceiling line that is to receive the stone treatment, and divide as close as possible to the nearest measurement of 14" (35.6 cm), which is the height of the blocks. Example: a 92" (2.3 m) space would have approximately six and a half blocks. However, it is undesirable to have a block cut in half. To get seven full blocks, divide the desired width by 7 to yield the ideal size for the blocks. Transfer this odd measurement to a stick, and mark the increments lightly on the wall, starting from the ceiling line down.

4. For the dark grout, mix a small amount of the mother glaze with 2 parts fast-drying glazing liquid, and add a few drops of water. Lower-open-time glazing liquids will dry quickly, so they can be worked over sooner for adding grout details in the cross direction. Place spacers on a large level to offset it from the wall. Find the first reference point below the ceiling, and place the level against it, making sure the level's bubble registers true for horizontal. Grout the wall with the liner. Make the horizontal grout line as long as possible before reloading and continuing. Do not repeatedly paint over the grout line, as it will become very dark. Continue for the entire room.

5. Register the points for the vertical grout lines just below the ceiling line, starting in an inconspicuous corner. Use a stick marked with the proper increments. Eighteen-inch (45.7 cm) -long stone blocks are measured in 9" (22.9 cm) increments, as each course of stone is staggered.

6. Starting at the ceiling, plumb the level true, and use it as the brush's guide against the marked points. Paint the vertical grout lines. Grout a stone course vertically, skip the course below it for the stagger, and continue the grout again on the next course down. Finish to the floor.

7. Move to the next point and start the vertical grout by skipping the first course and picking up the second and fourth courses down. Continue to create a staggered layout.

8. When the entire room is grouted, add a highlight. Cut a linen white base coat with an equal part of white paint and a bit of water. Using the level as a guide or painting free hand, paint the L-shaped highlight accent. Do not add glaze to the linen-white, as a transparent white will disappear when dry.

For horizontal grout lines, always paint the highlight white below the dark grout line. For vertical grout lines, choose either side of the dark grout line, but be consistent around the room once you have made your choice.

VARIATIONS

• For real texture on your faux stone, lay out the stone grid with a pencil over an appropriately colored base coat. Tape the grout lines with a ¼" (6 mm) -wide racing car tape purchased at an auto store. Texture-paint the entire surface, removing the tape promptly to expose the recessed grout line. Be sure to remove the grouting tape before the dried texture seals the tape in. Let the surface dry completely and then paint and glaze it, to add interest.

look twice: trompe l'oeil

Trompe l'oeil techniques create a three-dimensional effect. Simple additions of light and shadow make faux finishes appear real. Simple light and shadow elements, combined with layout skills and single process finishes, produce astounding results.

This garden trellis brings the outside in all year around. The light shadowing on the underside, combined with a background blue sky, provides a happy home for local plants and butterflies. See Technique Tutorial, page 160.

The mahogany trim and paneling throughout is in the red color family. The red is softened by a classic combination of green sueding on the walls. The orange tones of the copper ceiling construction mesh easily and provide a plausibly realistic color for the color grouping. Low, ceiling-down lighting was carefully factored in when sampling this finish. The ground, stencil pattern, and its painted shadows come to life in a narrow range of contrasts that was determined with careful mixing and calibration. See Technique Tutorial, page 163.

An overall color-washed glazing job was followed by grout placement. Many of the stones were then taped and further glaze-processed in several, soft-contrasting formulas. A collection of slightly different stones was accompanied by a similar treatment on the niche moldings. For a tutorial on the cut and dressed stone technique, see page 148.

A color-washed background of a deep, burnt-orange glaze over a yellow ochre base was further distressed with some light, negative veining. A dark accent in the grout recesses adds realism, as does sectioning of smaller cut stones around the muraled arch opening.

A high-contrast grout-to-ground combination works in the limited geometry of its placement. The strong lines of the stone treatment provide a foil for the soft curves of the stair stringers. Crown molding and above-the-stair wall finishes allow the faux stone to make a big impression.

Framing this window with wood-grained shutters and the wine bottle grouping place the European street scene squarely in the distance. Muralists find devices such as these necessary to establish the illusion of depth. Broken-back stucco reveals small dressed stone, creating a companion decorating motif with restrained impact in other parts of the room.

Broken-back stucco allows stone to frame an exploration of Egypt, without ever leaving home. The stone construction on the wall follows the tutorial layout, except for the variation in the height of the courses.

A peaceful pastoral scene, framed with stone and trellis, creates an illusion of space. Extra glaze steps in both elements reinforce a three-dimensional quality.

Faux-finished walls segue to a window mural, which creates distance for this modestly sized bedroom. The carefully laid out and painted window mullions complete the separation of room from sky. Carefully considered highlights and shadows, including the short shadows at the sides of the window, make this a powerful illusion.

Monochrome color schemes can be called upon for restful decoration. A dark mother color can be tinted up with a warm white, and shaded with raw umber to mix the palette. This idyllic landscape disappears in a haze and creates the illusion of space for a small sitting area by filling in the entire wall. A canvas painting of a similar scene does not have the same effect because the frame on the painting limits the deceit of distance.

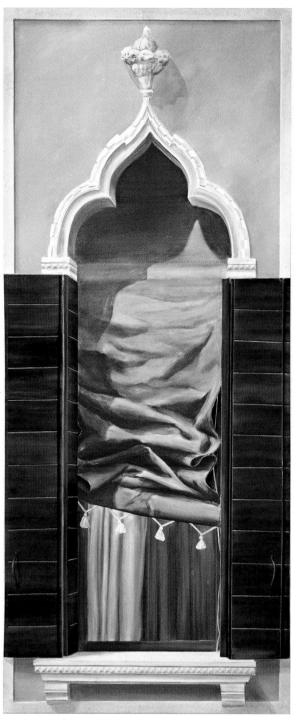

Look once, look twice, and keep touching to convince your eyes. Here is some real faux. Trompe l'oeil shadows and highlights create moldings where there are none. A door pull says, "Open me," but this is just nice wood graining on a flat surface.

Good faux finishers learn their textures from the study of natural materials such as stone, fabric, and wood. That knowledge combines with an understanding of light and shadow to make the illusions of trompe l'oeil.

Patrick Kirwin, UNITED STATES

Drapery is an ever-popular painted device for trompe l'oeil painters. The earliest record of a wacky window treatment concerns the ancient Greek master Zeuxis, whose antics come to us only in legend. Zeuxis was matched in a competition, where a curtain was presented on stage during the contest. The crowd agitated for an unveiling to see the painted scene behind the cloth. Nothing happened, and they grew impatient…only gradually realizing there was no painting behind, and that the drape itself was his entry .

In a more recent era, Napoleon and his generals inspired a French passion draping walls with real fabric, in imitation of the First Empire's elaborate military tents, became a decorative mania. Wallpaper manufacturers joined in printing the trend with ever-more-detailed drapery panels.

Gathered fabric was stretched from rods with swags, cording, and fringe, all on a double roll.

Printed drapery panels fashions leaped across the Atlantic and established themselves in the United States, where designers eventually added other trompe l'oeil elements such as wainscot and dado moldings, which were shadowed for a faux relief. Painters joined that party; a large painting by the early American master Charles Willson Peale of Philadelphia features a superb curtain partially drawn aside, allowing an intriguing glimpse of his natural history museum.

Trompe l'oeil manias come and go, and then come again. The devices are not new. Creased currency, watches with broken glass, gathered fabrics, and torn paper were here before, with messages such as careless spending, lost time, and hidden mysteries.

Patrick Kirwin continues trompe l'oeil traditions with the necessary sense of humor and skill for the detail such work demands. Kirwin's interest in fabrics began with canvas-size paintings, such as of a woman's gossamer dress hanging from a wall, or an old coat with details of the rips and wears it accumulated warming someone through their years. The objects shed some light on their owners, but leave us curious for more information.

Kirwin's mastery of fabrics led to commissions of two-story-high wall treatments. Faux methods remain important tools, especially when a curio grouping might be set on a wood-grained background, or the liner of a jacket receives a textured weave built up with steel-comb methods.

Kirwin ran out of real windows on this commission, so he included his own fenestration. Drapes tied back expose diaphanous curtains. The transparent nature of such fabrics, water, and glass are rendered with an advanced mastery of the glaze medium. This trompe l'oeil work left his client anticipating Christmas even on the hottest day in July.

Left: Kirwin has entertained numerous drapery commissions in recent years. Huge, painted treatments bracket this fireplace, pulled back with tasseled ties, as real drapes. Shadowing in the folds, cornice boxing, and an interruption of the fabric pattern by the folds convince the viewer that this is the real thing.

Below: A Chesapeake Bay inlet painted from wall to wall cheers viewers on the gloomiest day. Faux finishes for textures in the rowboat wood, and transparent glaze manipulation for the clouds to the horizon, are favored tools in Kirwin's paint kit.

trellises and tiles

COLOR FORMULA: linen white (base coat, top left), midtone blue (color for coloring glaze concoction, top right), orange and blue (for mixing trellis shadow color, bottom left), mixed gray, shadow glaze (below)

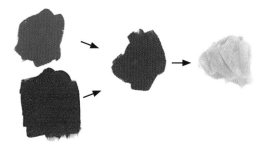

GARDEN PARTY

Historical wallpaper collections from the Cooper-Hewitt National Design Museum in New York City document the popularity of trellis motifs through time. Early nineteenth-century homes displayed expensive French latticework festooned with magnificent floral garlands rendered trompe l'oeil realistic with perfected block-printing techniques. Midbrow and budget customers of those days had their parlor gardens printed on more modestly priced domestic goods. Ending that century, the bamboo trellis was inspired by the all-things-Japanese mania influencing the public imagination.

Restorations in American colonial homes have uncovered trellis pattern paintings done by itinerant artisans in the century before wallpapers became available and put them out of a job.

Contemporary faux finishers use trellis patterns as full-room treatments, accent wall projects, and elements in mural constructions.

A trellis painted in a small powder room surprises and delights upon entry. Sunrooms and kitchen areas are also decorated attractively in this style. Real trellis lattice has been used in the home, but the painted version is preferable because it does not accumulate dust.

The simple garden trellis introduces a diamond pattern layout. Trompe l'oeil shadowing adds a realistic detail. The more artistically ambitious can use this trellis as the ground for a painted mural by adding birds, butterflies, and floral with vines.

Laying out the trellis is time-consuming work. Aligning the trellis pattern at corners can be a problem. A solid, length-long strip of lattice, painted in each corner and at the ceiling line (if the trellis continues on the ceiling), reduces the hair-pulling layout efforts.

To begin, draw a section of the proposed trellis on a piece of 6-ply railroad board. The width of the slats of the trellis is best kept at 1" (3.8 cm), which is the same as many painting tapes. The openings in the trellis might be 4" to 6" (10.2 to 15.2 cm) square. Cut out this trellis template. Keep a few of the cutout squares as an aid for laying out the trellis pattern on the wall; they help in checking the drift in the penciled pattern. Cut a few straight, long and short pieces of 1½" (3.8 cm) -wide board as valuable templates for transferring the pattern.

Base coat the walls with a linen white, eggshell paint and allow to dry.

MATERIALS

eggshell latex water-base paints: linen white (base coat), midtone blue (for mixing glaze concoction), orange

white latex semigloss

two acrylic glazing liquids (one with a long open time, one with a short open time)

TOOLS

basic layout and painting tools (see page 26)

carpenters' levels (various sizes)

trellis template

liner brush, ½" (1.2 cm) wide

high quality Chinex painter's cut brush, 1½" (3.8 cm) wide

orange core tape, 1½" (3.8 cm) wide

paint tray and sponge (for color-washing)

paper towels

INSTRUCTIONS

1. Color-wash the entire background with a midtone blue mixed with approximately 4 parts acrylic glaze. Keep the glazing irregular, with some areas denser than others. This sky glazing will be greatly eliminated later by the trellis pattern. Let dry.

2. Starting at the center of the blue-glazed wall, draw a soft plumb line from the top to the bottom of the room.

3. Align the trellis cutout template on the plumb line, below the ceiling line, and secure to the wall with tape. Lightly trace the trellis template as best you can, remove the template, and pencil in any misses with a ruler.

4. Move the trellis template adjacent to the traced area and secure it; trace the newly secured area. On large walls, additional plumb lines are useful to keep the layout true. Small variations and drifting of the pattern are acceptable. Use small pieces of templates and rulers to layout into corners. Be patient, and keep the pencil light!

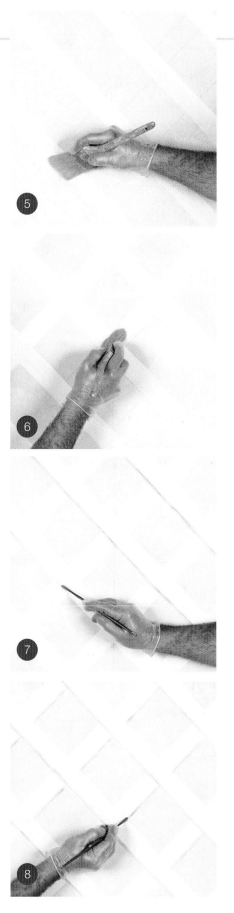

5. Use a painter's brush to paint all the lattice work with a white semigloss, painting all parallel slats first. A little water periodically mixed in the paint eases the flow from the brush. Paint over the layout pencil lines slightly, to eliminate them. Finish tight areas with artist brushes.

6. When the lattice is all painted in one direction and dry, paint in the opposite direction.

7. Take the blue mother glaze and add a few drops of orange, the complementary color, to mix a soft neutral gray. Increase the transparency of this mixed color by adding two more parts fast-drying acrylic glazing liquid. This shadow color should be thinned a bit with water to facilitate flow from the brush. Use a liner brush to paint the trellis only on the bottom edges where the shadow is away from the sun; continue around the entire room. Line the trellis in one direction and let dry. Keep the shadow color on the white painted trellis, not on the sky background.

8. Using a shorter line, complete the shadowing on the trellis openings. For ceiling shadows on the trellis (if the ceiling has been trellised), choose any direction (there is no top and bottom) and be consistent.

TRELLIS ADD-ONS

Windows, doorways, and other types of fancy embellishments can be added to trellises. For extra impact and a lot of additional time painting, the white trellis can be faux finished with a wood-grained technique.

BRONZE CEILING TILE

Use trompe l'oeil shadowing to create a fine imitation with mica paint metallics.

Picture an old time, small-town apothecary with pressed-tin ceiling tiles. That subtle relief delighted Victorians, along with similar embossed wall covering products such as anaglypta and lincrusta.

The bronze tones of the ceiling construction (shown at right and on page 151) mesh easily and provide a plausibly realistic color for the grouping. Low, ceiling-down lighting was carefully factored in when sampling this finish. The ground, stencil pattern, and its painted shadows come to life in a narrow range of contrasts, which was determined with careful mixing and calibration.

A baroque pattern is drawn on tracing paper and then filled out by folding and tracing the pattern for 1' (.3 sq m) -square motif, which is the size of the ceiling tiles.

Squares are taped off and glazed with a soft shadow overall. The baroque-inspired pattern is stenciled with an antique bronze base coat, leaving the positive pattern in antique bronze relief. An offset, harder shadow stencil carefully registered to the positive pattern makes the relief pop. Some straight shadows are done with a liner brush, which establishes the edges of the tiles.

Antique bronze metallic paint and a shadow formula in several transparencies make this deception from a simple color palette.

A good primer-sealer prepares the ceiling against ripping when the extensive taping is removed. Keep in mind that touch-ups on metallic grounds are particularly unforgiving.

NECK REST

Decorating ceilings can be painful; avoid a stiff neck with frequent rests and stretches.

MATERIALS

water-base paints: metallic mica paints; antique bronze (base coat and highlights); English brown (for shadow glazes); raw umber acrylic paint (for shadows); flat latex undercoat (tinted)

TOOLS

basic layout and painting tools (see page 26)

long straightedge

templates (for ceiling tile layout)

tile pattern (for tile stencils)

Mylar (for highlight and shadow stencils)

orange-core tape, 1" (2.5 cm) and 1½" (3.8 cm) wide

liner brush

sponge and tray (for color-washing)

paper towels

COLOR FORMULA Left to right: antique bronze, English brown, tinted flat latex primer

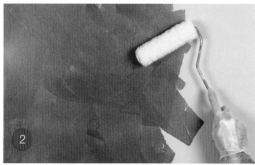

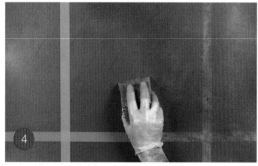

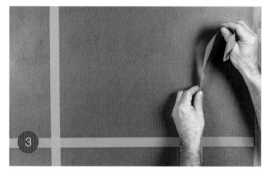

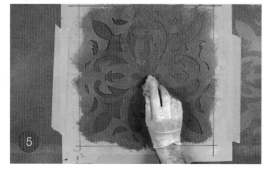

INSTRUCTIONS

1. Over a quality primer, paint the ceiling with one coat of tinted, flat paint that approximates the antique bronze metallic. An exaggerated contrast is shown in the photo.

2. When the paint is dry, paint several coats of antique bronze metallic paint to provide an opaque ground. Note that regular painting with metallics is a bit tricky, so read the directions carefully.

3. For the layout, find the middle of the ceiling and draw a 15" (38.1 cm) -square grid, parallel to the walls, over the entire ceiling. Penciling must be a bit vigorous to register the lines on such a dark ground. The pencil lines will remain as the narrow cracks visible between tiles on a real ceiling. Mask the entire ceiling grid with 1" (2.5 cm) tape, centering the tape on the grid lines. Tape the entire ceiling in one direction before taping across in the opposite direction. This will speed the tape removal. The final tile size will be 14" (35.6 cm) -square when the 1" (2.5 cm) tape is applied on all sides.

4. Glaze all the exposed squares with the transparent shadow glaze of 1 part English Brown mixed to 8 parts acrylic glazing liquid, using a dense artificial sponge to stipple it on as evenly as possible. Leave the tape in position until the end of the project.

5. Position each glazed square, using the corner registers on the snowflake stencils. Working with at least half a dozen prepared stencils will allow for faster work. Partnering, with one person setting and one striking, also works well for larger projects. Strike the stencils with the original antique bronze metallic base coat in the dense stipplelike manner of the previous step. Remove the stencil as you go. This step simply reestablishes the base coat eliminated in the first glazing step. The baroque floral-like pattern is now seen as a highlight. It is immaterial how this pattern is placed on the ground, as it is symmetrical in all directions.

6. For the accent-shadow color, mix 1 part artists' fluid acrylic raw umber paint to 4 parts glazing liquid. Use a liner brush against the positioned tape to paint the linear shadow. The shadow is painted on two sides of the square only and opposite to the position of the shadow of the snowflake stencil. Study the illustration carefully to understand the relation of the shadows. Every square must be shadowed on the same two sides. A patented lining tool marketed for car striping can be used to make quick work of this difficult task.

7. Use the corner registers to position the dark shadow stencil, which is slightly offset from the highlight pattern, and stipple with the accent-shadow glaze. Unlike the snowflake pattern, all shadow patterns must be registered in the same direction so that the cast shadows all align in one direction. A register arrow is placed on all shadow stencils, and attention is paid to always having the arrow point in the same direction.

8. Remove tape with great care to avoid damaging the surface.

Use the snowflake method to create a stencil pattern.

stencil making

Transfer a pattern to a decorated surface with stencils in a dependable and time-saving manner. The use of stencil patterns over faux-finished grounds is in vogue, such as a damask pattern repeating on a previously fauxed color wash.

Add the detailing steps of highlight and shadow to stenciled work with artist brushes to get spectacular results in a hand-painted look.

Silk stencils were first discovered in ancient tombs in China. Japanese craftsman stenciled from the 1700s in unbelievably complex and intricate designs. Victorians embellished walls, ceilings, and trim with a myriad of mostly classical motifs. Those motifs were in a large part inspired by the 1856 publication of *Grammar of Ornament* by Owen Jones, which continues to be a primary source in the present stencil revival. Greek key motifs and Baroque flourishes dominate today's stencil pattern choices, replacing the recent cow-and-chicken era that prejudiced so many against the use of stencils.

glossary

ANAGLYPTA: a late-Victorian-era, embossed wallpaper

ANTIQUED: finished to look old

BASE COAT: the first coat of paint, applied before glaze

BLOOM: cloudiness in a clear finish that is caused by trapped moisture

BRECCIA: broken chunks of stone in a marble matrix

CHINOISERIE: a style of traditional Chinese painting

COMPLEMENTARY COLORS: colors opposite from each other on the color wheel, such as red and green.

CONCOCTION: a mixture of glazing liquid and paint

CRATERING: the effect of air bubbles trapped in a concoction that surface and pop open

DISTRESS: in painting, to manipulate a glazed surface with a technique

EMERY: extremely-fine-grit black sandpapers

FAUX BOIS: a French term for a realistic imitation of wood

FAUX MARBE: a French term for a realistic imitation of marble

GRIDDING UP: enlarging a pattern or drawing to a large size

GROUND: the surface on which one is painting

HAND: the difference in touch or style in crafted items

HARLEQUIN: a diamond pattern usually rendered in light and dark tones

KNOCK DOWN: textured finishes that are passed over with a trowel to depress high relief

LAP: the overlapping area where a wet glaze is distressed against already applied glaze

LINCRUSTA: a linoleum-like Victorian wallcovering with moderate relief, which often receives painted effects

MARBLEIZING: using marble as inspiration, but not exact replication

MONOCHROME: painting in shades and tints of the same color

MOTHER COLOR: A color that is altered by variations such as tints, shades, and coloring of glazes and applied to create a finish.

MUD: an affectionate name for thicker-body formulas such as texture paints

OPEN TIME: the time during which a glazing concoction can be distressed

PALETTE: a group of colors used together in a decorating scheme

PICKED OUT: on relief surfaces, using techniques that emphasize the high parts

POLYCHROME: a multicolored combination

RAILROAD BOARD (also called oak tag): a dense, water-resistant board used in many faux techniques

REGISTER: in stenciling, to line up a pattern with previously established points

SCROLLER: a small, detail brush used in floral painting

STRAP DOWN: when a glaze grabs a surface and cannot be removed with solvent

STRIKE: the impression made when a stencil pattern is painted

TINT: to add white to any color; however, tinting a paint often means adding a colorant, thus making for a confusion of terms

TRANSFER: to place a pattern on a surface where it will be painted

TROMPE L'OEIL: a French term meaning "to fool the eye" with three-dimensional painting techniques

UNIVERSAL PIGMENTS: concentrated paint colorants that are compatible with any base

VARNISH: a generic term that makes reference to clear finishes of a wide spectrum

WOOD-GRAINING: using wood as an inspiration, but not in exact replication

contributing artists

Sigmund Aarseth
2940 Heggenes, Norway
(47) 905 55581
Post@sigmundaarseth.com
www.sigmund-aarseth.com
Page 60–61

Karen Arcand Johnson
Arcand Johnson Design
2555 Valley View Avenue East
Maplewood, MN 55119 USA
(651) 739-8757
arcandjohnsondesign@comcast.net
www.archandjohnsondesign.com
Page 122

Annabel Armstrong
Surface, LLC
1516 North 27th Street
Boise, ID 83702 USA
(208) 344-0752
surface@crazybunny.com
Page 141 (bottom)

Laura Ashleigh
Artistic Finishes LLC
2803 E. Belleview Place, Studio 8
Milwaukee, WI 53211 USA
(414) 915-3377
laura@ArtisticFinishes.biz
www.artisticfinishes.biz
Page 103 (bottom); 138 (bottom)

Martin Benad
Atelier Benad
Woerth Strasse 25
87667 Muenchen, Germany
(44) 49 89 48957372
atelier@benad.com
www.atelier-benad.de and www.benad.com
Page 156 (top); 157 (right)

Christopher J. Audley
Painting by Design Inc.
60 Thoreau Street PMB 195
Concord, MA 01742 USA
(617) 957-0414
cjaudley@hotmail.com
www.paintingbydesign.us
Page 17; 74 (top); 130 (top); 107

Kari Barron
Make A Scene Designs by Kari Barron
38101 Murrieta Creek Drive
Murrieta, CA 92562 USA
(951) 677-1736
info@makeascenedesigns.com
www.makeascenedesigns.com
Page 57 (top); 104 (right)

Muriel Calderon
36 Prince Street
Red Hook, NY 12571 USA
(845) 758-1040
murielcalderon@downunderfaux.com
www.muriel.calderon@downunderfaux.com
Page 34; 89

Mats Carlsson
Palm Fine Arts
Södra Promenaden 39
602 34 Norrköping, Sweden
(46) 11 36 69 50
info@palmfinearts.nu
www.palmfinearts.nu
Page 157 (left)

Lisa A. Cicalese McMillen
Cica Lisa Designs
15 Kingswoods Drive
New Hope, PA 18938 USA
(215) 862-1665
cicalisa@verizon.net
www.cicalisadesigns.com
Page 125; 155

Neil R. Clapp
Imagine Decorative Paintworks
24 Shady Lane Drive
Wilmington, MA 01887 USA
(978) 988-1670
neilclapp@verizon.net
www.PDCA.org/imagine
Page 59 (bottom)

Tania Corse
Corse Creations
48–17 42nd Street, #1C
Sunnyside, NY 11104 USA
(917) 319-4308
tania@corsecreations.com
www.corsecreations.com
Page 72 (bottom); 154 (bottom)

Connie and Stephen R. Cotita
Studio Abbellire
103 Country Lane
West Monroe, LA 71291 USA
(318) 547-3726
ranman@cotita
www.studioabbellire.com
Page 56 (top); 66 (bottom, left); 70 (bottom)

Tom Dean
Dean Decorative Painting
219 Hillcrest Drive
Kitty Hawk, NC 27949 USA
(252) 255-2035
tom@deandecorativepainting.com
www.deandecorativepainting.com
Page 87 (bottom); 88 (bottom, left)

Victor DeMasi
Monarch Painting
10 Simpaug Turnpike
Redding, CT 06896 USA
(203) 448-0106
victormonarch@yahoo.com
monarchpainting.net
All other work shown

Laine Discepoli
MissElaineous Studio
18 Village Square
Glendale, OH 45246 USA
(513) 533-3289
laine@misselaineous.net
www.misselaineous.net
Page 57 (top)

Janie Ellis
Anything But Plain, Inc.
12539 Duncan, Suite D
Houston, TX 77066 USA
(281) 444-2070
abp@flash.net
www.anythingbutplain.com
Page 101; 102; 139

Russell A. Erwin
Erwin Art, LLC
4010 Hawick Drive
Houston, TX 77084 USA
(713) 247-0073
russell@russellerwin.com
www.russellerwin.com
Page 12; 71; 123 (top); 124 (left)

Irene Gindera
Gindera Painting and Decorative Finishes
P. O. Box 198
Rifton, NY 12471 USA
(845) 532-5615
gindera-irene@hotmail.com
Page 151; 163

Bill Graffis
Alla Prima Studies
1516 Waverly Street
Houston, TX 77008 USA
(832) 654-3289
bgraffi1@ix.netcom.com
www.allaprimastudios.com
Page 52 (top)

James H. Hajny, Sr.
James Hajny LLC
24625 August Lane
Lake Zurich, Il 60047 USA
(847) 606-9119
jameshajny@comcast.net
Page 152 (top)

Lizbeth Harrison
Rebecca Kunimoto
Wild Horse Studio
180 Old Alabama Place
Roswell, GA 30076 USA
(770) 317-0777
wildhorsestudio2@aol.com
www.wildhorsestudio.biz
Page 141 (top); 142

Patricia Henning
Fabulous Finishes, Inc.
54049 Huntington Drive
Shelby Twp., MI 48316 USA
(313) 318-6511
pattyhenning@comcast.net
www.fabfinisher.com
Page 118 (bottom)

Martitia (Tish) Louise Inman
Gotcha Covered
1151 Lakewood Drive
Gallatin, TN 37066 USA
(615) 230-8689
igotcha@infionline.net
www.igotchacovered.com
Page 73 (bottom); 105; 118 (top); 126

Dena M. Jasinski
Fauxbulous Finishes by Dena Marie
N40 West 22750 Crescent Drive
Pewaukee, WI 53072 USA
(262) 695-2327
djasinski2@wi.rr.com
Page 54 (bottom); 86; 90 (bottom)

Patrick Kirwin
500 S. Walter Reed Drive, #23
Arlington, VA 22204 USA
(703) 521-9037
pkirwin@earthlink.net
www.patrickkirwin.com
Page 158–159

Yaeko Kurimata
Faux Arts Design
1-3-23 Higashikoiwa Edogawaku
Tokyo, Japan 133-0052
(81) 3 5668 7369
yaeko@faux-arts-design.biz
Page 144–145

Diane Lauer-Harrison
ILLUDERE, Decorative Painting & Design
2923 Old San Jose Road
Soquel, CA 95073 USA
(831) 464-1415
dlauer@illudere.com
Page 72 (top); 121 (bottom)

Alyse Leventhal
Amy Leuenthal
DoubleTake Designs
3017 Stonehaven
Springfield, OH 45503 USA
(518) 879-3050
doubletake2@hotmail.com
Page 32

Richard Lazenby
Lazenby's Decorative Arts Studio
6128 Double Oak Way
Birmingham, AL 35242 USA
(205) 281-5273
riklazenby@charter.net
Page 90 (top); 153

Marilyn MacLeod
Lee Design
21 Verndale Street
Brookline, MA 02446 USA
(617) 504-1811
m@leedesign.biz
www.leedesign.biz
Page 57 (bottom); 65 (top); 87 (top)

Alejandro Markus
Painting by Alejandro
17 Rocky Glen Road, Apt. 3
Danbury, CT 06810 USA
(203) 953-9616
amarkus@comcast.net
Page 68

Sally P. Masteller
Custom Art West
11701 Heathcliff Drive
Santa Ana, CA 92705 USA
(714) 669-0269 or (888) 774-4278
customartwest@sbcglobal.net
www.customartwest.com
Page 58 (top); 88 (bottom, right)

André Martinez
Awendan
4352 Eliot Street
Denver, CO 80211 USA
(720) 260-8858
contact@awendan.com
www.awendan.com
Page 53; 75; 143

Karen McClain
P.O. Box 1361
Tacoma, WA 98401-1361 USA
(253) 572-9320
kmvisuals@yahoo.com
www.karenmcclain.com
Page 56 (bottom)

Jeff Monsein
Splat Paint
2446 West Prospect Road
Tampa, FL 33629 USA
(813) 253-3700
info@splatpaint.com
www.splatpaint.com
Page 74 (bottom); 120

Lucretia Moroni
Fatto a Mano
50 West 28th Street, Suite 1403
New York, NY 10001 USA
Phone: (212) 686-4848
lucet@ix.netcom.com
fatto-a-mano.com
Page 128–129

Joanne Nash
Joanne Nash Decorative Painting
101 Hunters Lane
Gladys, VA 24554 USA
(434) 283-4861
jjnash57@yahoo.com
www.joannenash.com
Page 123 (bottom); 140 (top); 154 (top)

Valerie Naulleau
Atelier de Lili
5 allée du Pont Noget
85200 Fontenay-Le-Cohte, France
(33) 682 69 2853
vnaulleau@yahoo.fr
Page 54 (top); 156 (bottom)

Lotta Olsson
Palm Fine Arts
Södra Promenaden 39
602 34 Norrköping, Sweden
Phone: (46) 11 36 69 50
lotta@palmfinearts.nu
www.palmfinearts.nu
Page 20; 49; 108–109

Leonard Pardon
Pardon Studio Inc.
5600 NE 5th Avenue
Miami, FL 33137 USA
Phone: (305) 758-5828
pardonfauxpar@yahoo.com
www.pardonstudio.com
Page 140 (bottom); 152 (bottom)

Mary Patterson
Painted by Patterson, LLC
150 Pond Road
Felton, PA 17322 USA
(717) 246-8060
mary@paintedbypatterson.com
www.paintedbypatterson.com
Page 43 (top); 91 (bottom); 100 (top);
106 (bottom); 127

Marc Potocsky
MJP Studios
241 Branford Road, 254
North Branford, CT 06471 USA
(203) 488-1265
mjpfaux@aol.com
www.mjpfaux.com
Page 70 (top); 124 (right)

Tatiana Rugers
Creative Ambience
2507 West Morrison Avenue
Tampa, FL 33629 USA
(813) 390-4120
enophilefl@cs.com
www.creative-ambience.com
Page 138 (top)

Jean-Luc Sable
Jean Sable Mural Art
21 rue Saint Louis
78000 Versaille, France
(33) 139 209 976
jean-sable@orange.fr
www.jean-sable.com
Page 76–77; 78

Wanda Sadowska
Wanda's Creations
8305 Winnipesaukee Way
Lake Worth, FL 33467 USA
(561) 716-2516
leslawsadowski@comcast.net
Page 55; 106 (top)

Greg Sargema
Modern Masters
9380 San Fernando Road
Sun Valley, CA 91352 USA
(818) 683-0201
info@modernmastwsrsinc.com
www.modernmasters.com
Page 15; 88 (top)

Nina Slezak
Celestial Interiors
58 Morningside Avenue
Toronto, ON M6S 1C5 Canada
(416) 604-2276
celestialinteriors@rogers.com
www.celestialinteriors.com
Page 151; 163

Doreen Sharabati
Doreen Designs
1242 Cordova Road
Fort Lauderdale, FL 33316 USA
(954) 760-9569
DORISAM123@gmail.com
Page 119; 121 (top)

Ronnie Soubra
AMZAJ
Furn El Hayek,
Masabni Bldg. Asharfieh
Beriut, Lebanon
961 3 636 860
tunamina@yahoo.com and
amzajitos@yahoo.com
www.smcinteriors.net
Page 16; 92–93

Mozelle Spencer
Mozelle by Design
3030 80th Ave S.E., #309
Mercer Island, WA 98040 USA
(206) 755-7721
mozellebydesign@hotmail.com
www.mozellebydesign.com
Page 11; 100 (bottom); 113 (top)

Eric Spiegel
Spiegel's Decorative Finishes
2166 Long Boat Drive
Naples, FL 34104 USA
Phone: (239) 262-5255
eric@spiegelsdecorativefinishes.com
www.spiegelsdecorativefinishes.com
Page 31 (bottom); 73 (top); 91 (top)

Elizabeth Adrienne van Dooren
The House That Faux Built
7317 Castleberg Court
Alexandria, VA 22315 USA
Phone: (571) 239-6656
chair@fauxhouse.com
www.fauxhouse.com
Page 85; 94

George Zaffle
Luthea Thomas
Zaffle Painting Studios
P.O. Box 4066
Truckee, CA 96160 USA
(530) 582-8001
zaffle@mindspring.com
www.zaffle.com
Page 104 (left)

resources

Paint Products and Supplies

The following suppliers manufacture or distribute most of the paint products featured in the technique tutorials this book.

BENJAMIN MOORE & COMPANY (www.benjaminmoore.com) house paints are useful for base coating and mother-colors. Their acrylic glaze is very fast-drying, making it a poor choice for most wall techniques, but an excellent choice for hand-painted techniques and murals.

THE FLECTO COMPANY (www.rustoleum.com) is a great choice for their Diamond brand clear finishes (varnish).

Go to **GOLDEN ARTIST COLORS, INC.** (www.goldenpaints.com) for Satin Acrylic Glazing liquid, a workhorse among water-base glazes with a long open time. Golden fluid acrylic paints are artist-style paints, which can be used to alter larger batches of more economically priced house paint.

MODERN MASTERS (www.modernmasters.inc.com) has a wonderful line of mica-base metallic paints as well as Venetian plasters. Their parent company, **ZINSSER** (www.zinsser.com), has an excellent selection of primers in various bases, including the white shellac product known as B-I-N.

PEARL PAINT COMPANY (www.pearlpaint.com) is a mail-order source for 6-ply railroad board and stencil-making Mylar, as well as a number of specialty tools.

PRATT AND LAMBERT (www.prattandlambert.com) oil-glazing liquid is a good choice for oil-base glazing concoctions.

MELANIE ROYALS (www.modellodesigns.com) offers a fine assortment of stencil patterns and useful techniques.

recommended reading

Books

The Art of Faux by Pierre Finkelstein, 1997, Watson-Guptil Publications, a division of BPI Communications, Inc.

This book offers extensive information on materials and methods by one of Europe's finest craftsmen.

Professional Painted Finishes by Ina Brosseau Marx, Allen Marx, and Robert Marx, 1991, Watson Publishing

This book includes excellent illustrated techniques and a guide to the base colors necessary for particular finishes. Discussions of glaze formulas in this volume are dated to the mostly oil-base era; more user-friendly, water-base formulas can be substituted.

The House That Faux Built by Adrienne van Dooren, 2007, East Cambridge Press

This designer showcase illustrates how a group of talented, contemporary faux artisans made their imaginations come alive.

Period Rooms in the Metropolitan Museum of Art by Amelia Peck, 1996, the Metropolitan Museum of Art.

Not sure what to paint? In this book, cruise dozens of historic treatments for furniture, fabrics, and decorative arts in their architectural surroundings.

Wallpaper in America: From the Seventeenth Century to World War I, by Catherine Lynn, 1980, The Barra Foundation, Inc.

Wallpaper and painted home decoration are intimately connected. This classic offers historic perspective with interesting discussions on the manufacture of wallpaper, which was derived from stencil techniques. An extensive visual survey of wallpaper fragments provides ideas as well as a cohesive sense of historic style.

American Decorative Wall Painting 1700–1850 by Nina Fletcher Little, 1952, Studio Publication

Explore the past and discover the wonderful creativity of our long-departed kindred spirits. This fascinating treatment reaps many rewards with ideas from the past for the job of tomorrow.

The Grammar of Ornament by Owen Jones, first published in 1856 by Day & Son, London; First American Edition in 2001 by the Ivy Press Limited

All patterns are copyright-free in this extensively used guide. Every painter I know owns this volume, and a lion's share of stencils available from current suppliers originated here.

The Painted House by Graham Rust, 1988, Alfred A. Knopf

Full of eye candy, this book put the imaginations of today's top muralist "on the page."

Magazines

American Painting Contractor (www.paintmag.com)

This trade magazine includes this author's column, "Decorators Corner."

The Faux Finisher (www.fauxfinishermagazine.com)

Discover where to learn real faux; also includes professional reviews of products and in-depth school listings.

The International Salon of Decorators

The history of the current Salon dates back to the early 1990s, when a modest international gathering took place in Kuurne, Belgium. Alfred Marrecau, a noted grand master of the brush, initiated the gathering, which was sponsored by the Belgium Independent Painters Society.

Salon members call themselves exclusively "decorators." This is the European concept of an artisan who takes his skill beyond simple execution (and replication) to actually invest in how the skills are implemented in design.

The Salon manifesto references the ancient Schilderers Guild of Europe, which is more than one thousand years old. Ancient Schilderers worked in paint and gold leaf, and are known to have decorated the shields of Viking warriors. Current Salon members include decorators who are working on commissions at Versailles and Westminster Palace.

The Salon gathers annually at varying international locations, where the decorators display their painted panels, demonstrate their skills, and lecture for one another's benefit and edification. Recent gatherings, as the events are called, were held in Oslo, Norway; Utrecht, Holland; and Chicago.

The Salon continues to evolve and expand, although entry is by invitation and rigorous review only. Members attempt to reach new heights of refinement in painted finishes with each gathering. Each gathering exceeds the last in inspiration and skill of technique.

A recent Salon in Denmark used the theme "Land of Fairy Tales," and members imagined, in paint, otherworldly landscapes of inlaid marbles and Hans Christian Andersen memorabilia. Another recent gathering celebrated kings, queens, and jacks in a tour de force of trompe l'oeil. (Many works were spirited away for a three-month display at the M. C. Escher Museum of illusion.)

Salon days are open to the public. Only here can one view some of the greatest masters of painted deception at their task. The diversity of exhibition panels produced in demonstration of the theme is a celebration of the creative spirit.

Stencil Artisan League, Inc. (SALI)

Not only stencils, but all forms of faux finishing and murals form the core activities of this 3,000-member-plus organization dedicated to better living through paint. Their glossy magazine, *Artistic Stenciler,* features projects for all levels of skill, along with tutorials on the new products hitting the market. The SALI website gallery showcases hundreds of the best completed treatments. Here is the testimonial to members' skills and their willingness to share: the gallery is open to the public, providing lots of ideas for anyone's project.

Local SALI chapters meet regularly for educating and engaging in group philanthropic projects, such as murals for children's hospitals. This networking resulted in a recent effort, The House That Faux Built, where many members refurbished a house for sale and a published an eye-popping book of painted finishes, to raise money for the Hurricane Katrina victims.

SALI members meet each year in various U.S. locations for their annual convention. More than 500 members strong, attendees commandeer a hotel for a week of hands-on workshops, presentations, lectures, and a trade show where painting products of every persuasion are on display.

Recent convention speakers included *Paint Magic* author Jocasta Innes and famed architectural trompe l'oeil muralist Richard Haas, whose painted deceptions cover the entire sides of multistory buildings.

Master painters of every style and discipline offer more than one hundred classes at reasonable prices, all in one place: a weeklong University of Faux. The portfolio room displays members' work that is usually only seen during appointments in their hometowns. The SALI convention is a gathering of kindred spirits and electric energy.

photographer credits

All photography by Randy O'Rourke with the exception of the following:
John Aylward, 89
Ron Benton, 43; 91 (bottom); 100 (top); 106 (bottom); 127
Victor DeMasi, 28
William Garrow, 74 (bottom); 120
Joelle Mauroy, Jacques Postel, Baptiste Legatin, 7–78
Roanna Metowski, 4; 27 (top); 29; 31; 35; 36; 45 (bottom); 114–115
Katrina Mojzesz, 125; 155
Joyce Paisley, 54 (bottom); 86; 90 (bottom)
Sofia Paunovic, 20; 49; 108; 109; 157 (left)
Randall Perry, 73 (top); 91 (top)
Marc Potocsky, Justin Maturo, 70 (top); 124 (bottom)
Eric Roth, 57 (bottom); 65 (top); 87 (top)
Ron Ruscio, 53; 143

acknowledgments

Thanks goes first to Kristin Müller of the Brookfield Craft Center in Brookfield, Connecticut, who recommended me for the job of writing this book and then advised me how to go about it: get up and start writing at 5:00 a.m. every morning!

Patrick Kirwin, with his Salon connections and periodic encouragement, deserves special mention.

A great debt is owed my co-workers on painting projects for their dedication to often tedious and difficult tasks; the results of those tasks formed the basis of the how-to sections in these pages.

Thank you to the folks at Quarry Books for making this book possible, especially Rochelle Bourgault, my editor, who spearheaded the effort, patiently advised the ignorant (me), and introduced me to the mechanics of crafting a book, and Betsy Gammons who took me the final yards to the finish the line.

All the artists who generously contributed photos for the galleries—and others who submitted and were not included but who definitely qualified in the category of talent—deserve mention. They are all invited to paint my house.

My spouse, Roanna, as always through our years together, contributed selflessly with many small and large helpings too numerous to list. She gets double thanks.

All the wonderful clients in my more than thirty years behind the brush who had the confidence to let me practice on their homes. *Tusen Tak* to them, a thousand thanks, as they say in Norway.

Randy O'Rourke, the photographer for the tutorials and my beauty shots, took this book the final distance with his helpful advice and professional skills.

about the author

Victor DeMasi is the thirty-year owner of Monarch Painting, a decorative painting firm in Redding, Connecticut, which specializes in faux finishes and tromp l'oeil. His murals often feature natural history subjects, such as native wild flowers and butterflies. Clients are often delighted to find a painted monarch butterfly sitting on top of a window frame in an unlikely corner of their house. "Metamorphosis is our business" is the company's slogan.

DeMasi's name appears on the referral list maintained by the Connecticut Historical Trust. He has been contracted for historical painting-restoration projects for Yale University, the National Park Service, and the State of Washington. DeMasi is also known for his writing, teaching, and lecturing.

His work has been featured in *House and Garden,* the *New York Times, Yankee Magazine* and *Connecticut Magazine,* to name a few. He has authored more than ninety magazine articles, including pieces for *Fine Home Buildings* and *Fine Woodworking,* and is a major contributor to *The*

Readers Digest Book of Tools and Skills. He is a regular columnist for *American Painting Contractor* and *The Faux Finisher* magazine. He conducts workshops at his own studio, and also teaches regularly at the Brookfield Craft Center in Brookfield Connecticut, and at Stencil Artisan League (SALI) conventions. He has worked in more than one thousand residences.

In May 2002, DeMasi was honored with a membership in the International Salon of Decorators. DeMasi has participated and exhibited at recent SALI gatherings in the United States, Belgium, Norway, the Netherlands, and Denmark.

In his spare time, Victor DeMasi is a wetland conservation officer for his hometown of Redding and a research affiliate at the Yale Peabody Museum of Natural History in New Haven. He busies himself with preserving open space in town and preserving butterflies in the museum. His fieldwork with butterflies contributed almost one thousand citations to the recently published *Connecticut Butterfly Atlas.*

SELF-PORTRAIT OF ARTIST, APRIL 2007

Victor DeMasi has captured a fairy in the jar to add to his collection of butterflies. A Grimm thought, indeed.